THE

INDISPENSABLE WOMAN

Also by Ellen Sue Stern

EXPECTING CHANGE
The Emotional Journey Through Pregnancy

THE

INDISPENSABLE WOMAN

ELLEN SUE STERN

BANTAM BOOKS

NEW YORK · TORONTO · LONDON · SYDNEY · AUCKLAND

THE INDISPENSABLE WOMAN

A Bantam Book

Bantam paperback edition / October 1988
Bantam trade paperback edition / March 1991

Library of Congress Cataloging-in-Publication Data

Stern, Ellen Sue, 1954–
   The indispensable woman / Ellen Sue Stern.
     p. cm.
   Includes bibliographical references.
   ISBN 0-553-35231-8
   1. Women—Psychology. 2. Stress (Psychology) 3. Perfectionism
(Personality trait) 4. Success. I. Title.
HQ1206.S79 1991
155.6'33—dc20
                                     90-40215
                                        CIP

Published simultaneously in the United States and Canada

PRINTED IN THE UNITED STATES OF AMERICA

OPM   0 9 8 7 6 5 4 3 2 1

In memory of my beloved father-in-law, Lester Stern, who's still crossing his fingers and lighting candles in heaven.

ACKNOWLEDGMENTS

I acknowledge. Two words with a lot of power. To acknowledge—not merely to thank, but rather, to name, to show respect for what is real and true.

What's real and true about writing a book is that no one does it completely alone. People give in lots of different ways: Some people, especially those closest to the author, are expected to walk on eggshells, justify their criticisms, and sustain endless fascination for the subject. Other people are recruited in the name of research, their personal experiences transformed into case studies. Then there are the unwitting contributors, virtual strangers cornered at social gatherings and in the checkout line at the supermarket. They are the guinea pigs, the testing ground for new material.

To all who gave to this book, who cared about how it turned out and what it meant to me to write it, I express my profound gratitude. Beginning with the closest, I acknowledge Gary Stern, my husband, for giving this book its title, for careful editing of every word, and for sharing your home with this sometimes unwelcome and unwieldy guest.

To Zoe and Evan, I acknowledge your terrific patience in waiting for me to finish working so we could go play at Color Park. I hold you close and love you very, very much.

To Beverly, my editor—I have felt your caring and personal involvement throughout. It makes a real difference knowing the book is in good hands.

To my parents—Frank and Rosalie Kiperstin, and Jane Stern, your support and enthusiasm have been a constant source of support.

To my sister—Faith Schway, thank you for being there for me. I've really felt it.

To Jonathan and Wendy Lazear—my appreciation for your help in shaping the Indispensable Woman and for your ongoing encouragement and support on my behalf.

I acknowledge the contributions of the following friends:

Jan Magrane—for honest, thoughtful feedback given graciously.

Jill Edelstein—for careful, in-depth comments and for always remembering to ask how it was going.

Susan Boren—your insight has been a gift, your friendship a bonus.

Cindy Fishman—for being excited about my work and helping me remember why it mattered in the first place.

Ann Mond Johnson—for your positive energy and encouragement.

Rhoda Levin—for taking the time to help me sort out ideas and treating the project with love and respect.

Sara Tobias-Reich—for affirming me as an artist and helping me learn what to take seriously and what to laugh at.

Lauren Elkin—for telling me the truth, always. And for your warmth.

Ellen Levy—for your caring and thoughtful criticism.

Bonnie Dickel—for cheering me on and caring about the details.

Rebecca Rising—for your joyousness and for sharing your memories.

Kathlyn Stewart—for passionately confronting my ideas.

Sam Modenstein—for graciously sharing your home.

Debbie Hasko—for being genuinely supportive and interested.

Emily Hallock—for hosting a focus group and for your enthusiasm.

Katherine Mitchell—for your early support on the project.

Vicky Stewart—for your excitement and helpful feedback.

Finally, the book was written with the help of many women who participated in focus groups and interviews. From the bottom of my heart I acknowledge the contributions of: Jennifer Kaufenberg, Carol Redmond, Therese Casey, Rochelle Graves, Yvonne Cheek, Sara Strickland, Carla Ekdahl, Lonnie Helgeson, Paula Roe, Lucy Gerold, Becky McKenzie, Jayne Stuart, Kathleen McGoldrick, Dorothy Mosso, Alice Okrent, Mary Coleman, Dawn Graves, Cheryl Dickson, Marlene Forss, Sandra Lipsey, Barbara Chester, Nancy Hughs, Betty Ann Zeoli, Georgia Otis, Connie Grandahl, Barb Peterson, Nancy Blanchard, Judy Coley, Rhoda Weber, and the Reverend Canon Rona Harding.

CONTENTS

As our hands held before our eyes hide the tallest mountain, so the routine of everyday life keeps us from seeing the vast radiance and the secret wonders that fill our world.
—Chasidism, 18th century

THE

INDISPENSABLE WOMAN

INTRODUCTION

A few years ago, had someone called me an Indispensable Woman, I would have said, "Thank you." I would have considered it a compliment. Today, I know better.

For years I thought of myself as a high-achiever. But my expectations—which I extended whenever I came close to accomplishing my goals—made it impossible ever to feel satisfied with my success. Whatever I took on, I approached not with joy, but with perfectionism and grim resolution. I was driven by intense, self-imposed pressure. I wasn't able to enjoy the fruits of my labor or learn from my experience.

As an Indispensable Woman, I ran myself ragged. And was proud of it! I stacked one challenge on top of another, regardless of whether time and energy allowed. When I wasn't racing around filling each minute with activity, I turned the force of my attention on the other people in my life, with or without an invitation.

I applied the same standard of perfectionism to my family and friends. I presided over my husband Gary's involvements, criticizing when his pace or productivity lagged. When his share of responsibilities wasn't completed on *my* timetable, I'd simply take over, thus adding to my already teeming pile of demands. I treated my children like projects, efficiently managing and orchestrating their lives, often at the expense of their feelings.

There were numerous warning signs that I was in trouble. Friends, put off for the sixteenth time, questioned why I couldn't find five minutes to catch up. Tensions grew at home, and my work suffered as I committed to tighter and tighter deadlines.

At two A.M. one morning, I was frantically working at my computer. My three-year-old son Evan appeared in the kitchen bleary-eyed, thumb in mouth, clutching his beloved Raggedy Andy.

"What's wrong, honey?" I asked, one eye on the screen.

"Nothing. I'll just lie on the floor next to you until you're done," he replied. I felt guilty. But I still couldn't make myself stop.

Meanwhile, I complained about how much I had to do, how little time I had for myself, and how little help I got from anyone else. Deep inside, although I never would have admitted it, I sensed something had to change.

This book is about change. I have learned, both from my own experience and from the experience of hundreds of women, that it is possible to change. There is a way to be productive, successful, and fulfilled without making ourselves "indispensable." Without making ourselves sick.

But it won't happen without effort. Or time. It's taken years to become an Indispensable Woman. Undoing the patterns won't take place overnight. Long-term change requires looking honestly at our lives and realizing that it's nice to be needed, but not at the expense of our health, our happiness, and our sanity. It requires prioritizing and delegating, choosing what is and isn't essential to do. It means stopping long enough to feel our fatigue and notice the impending signs of burnout before they result in more serious and long-term harm. It means learning to ask for support and learning to relinquish control. Finally, it means realizing that the frantic pursuit of outward achievement and perfect results is counterproductive and, ultimately, self-destructive. Believing in our hearts that who we are is enough is the key to a more satisfying and balanced life.

All women today live with pressure: young women struggling with making the "right" career choices; single women forging a new path amid stubborn stereotypes; new mothers coping with isolation; growing numbers of women trying valiantly to integrate family and work; women passing through mid-life revisions of identity and relationships; older women trying to make peace with the inevitabilities of aging and mortality, and coming to terms with who they are and what they've made of their lives.

These pressures are real. Unquestionably, much of our stress comes from lack of support for women's changing roles. Despite the prevalence of two-income families, most women continue to take responsibility for social, domestic, and child-care demands, with only token participation from men. Although women account for forty-four percent of the work force, practical and emotional support for working mothers remains a drudgingly uphill battle. Pay inequity, job discrimination, and the absence of fully sanctioned maternity leave, socially supported childcare, and flexible work schedules inhibit women from realizing their full potential and make career paths more like obstacle courses.

Some women have it harder than others. Disability, lack of education, poverty, and racial prejudice—factors beyond an individual's control, and that dictate reality—create hardships beyond what other, more fortunate women cope with in their daily lives. There *are* women who are *truly* indispensable in some ways or for some period of time: the single mother who is the sole provider for her family; the devoted daughter, single-handedly caring for an ill and aging parent; the loyal friend who is "right there" during a serious crisis.

This book is *not* addressed to women who are genuine mainstays in difficult struggles and situations but who do not make a pattern of such behavior. Nor is it an attempt to confront the political and social structure that, by its failure to support women, contributes to our pressure.

My focus in writing this book is to identify how women make *themselves* indispensable, creating more pressure on top of what already exists. My goal is to illuminate why and how we perpetuate this addictive pattern, and show how to stop.

I am often asked, "What about men? Aren't men perfectionists too?" The answer is, yes, of course men cope with similar issues. And while I hope men find themselves in the pages of this book and benefit from it, I have written specifically to women for two reasons. First, because men, although they are often perfectionists, manifest it in different ways. In general, men are less approval-seeking and not nearly as "other-oriented" as women. Consequently, they aren't as apt to try to get their needs met by making themselves indispensable.

And, I have written from a female perspective because it is what I know best and care most about. I am expressly committed to helping women free themselves.

This book began as a personal search. For every answer, there have been new questions and deeper layers of understanding. Initially it was liberating simply to name "The Indispensable Woman," coining a phrase that for me was the first step in defining a pattern of behavior that had taken over my life. As I've shared my findings, I've come to see how pervasive and universal the problem is. As I've probed deeper and deeper, I've recognized what we get out of being indispensable as well as the enormous, inevitable costs.

I now know there is an alternative. It is my wish that as you read this book, you will gain strength and conviction to make your life your own. There is a good and right sense in which we *are* all indispensable. But we must peel away the layers of habit and conditioning in order to see how each of us is a unique and valuable human being. I hope this book will mark the way.

ONE

RUNNING
ON EMPTY

The spring of 1986 should have been among the happiest times of my life. The manuscript of my first book had been accepted, my kids were fine, and my mother was finally recovering after a long illness. I had much to feel thankful about and lots to look forward to.

But I wasn't happy. I was depressed and anxious; some mornings I had to talk myself into getting out of bed. Once up, I'd waste precious hours staring at my notebooks, my thoughts too muddled to write, occasionally starting another fresh list of things to get done. Although I was immersed in a new, stimulating project, it just felt like another weight on my shoulders. At my thirty-second birthday surprise party I pretended to have fun.

Inside, I was weary. Not physical fatigue, but emotional exhaustion, penetrating deep into my bones. I couldn't understand why I was so worn out. My life wasn't exactly relaxing, with two boisterous children, a husband, and a full-time career as a writer and director of a nonprofit organization. Still, I wouldn't have traded any of it, even at those times when I'd commiserate with a friend about always being in a rush or joke about sending my kids to boarding school in Switzerland.

So why couldn't I shake the increasing resentment, the fear that my best energy was being gobbled and used up? I was putting out more than I was taking in, and little by little the well was running dry.

I knew something was wrong. I just couldn't put my finger on it, until one afternoon when I was on my way to transport my daughter Zoe the three blocks from nursery school to the day-care home where she'd spend the rest of the day with her three-year-old brother.

As usual, I was late. It was the first warm day since early November, and we held hands as we picked our way to the car through mud-stained snowdrifts slowly melting into shallow puddles. It was our ritual for me to show up with a special treat, a Popsicle or a chocolate chip cookie, which Zoe slowly ate as we circled the block, stretching out our time together.

As we pulled up to the house, my eyes were drawn to the big bay window; through it I caught a glimpse that both reassured me and racked me with sadness: our day-care provider cradling my son Evan in her lap, rocking and cooing to him. I watched Zoe go up the walk and wave good-bye.

I got as far as the corner and pulled over. My mind was racing, vacillating between feeling pressured to hurry home and finish my work, and desperately wishing to turn back and collect my children. I sat sobbing in the car, torn and utterly lost. I couldn't figure out *where* I was supposed to be.

Although this was a relatively dramatic event, the same conflict occurred again and again. If I was taking care of my children, I'd panic over deadlines. When I was working, I'd agonize about my kids in day-care, certain they were dirty, or hungry, or wanting for affection. I'd drive myself crazy, feeling as though I should work harder, faster, and somehow make all of it fit. I became impatient and irritable, barking orders at my husband to finish household chores and cutting off friends mid-sentence when they called.

I was grasping at straws, trying to blame my feelings of stress on having an uncooperative husband, overly demanding kids, and a grueling schedule. But it wasn't true. Gary often takes on more than fifty percent of the housework, the kids seemed to understand when I couldn't be there for them, and for the first time in years, I was self-employed. If anything, my work pressures had lessened. Nonetheless, the seesaw of life's demands and remunerations was not evenly balanced. On the one side, too much responsibility. On the other, too little time, money, or support.

About this time, a plethora of magazine articles appeared, posing the question: Can women have it all? The answer: Not without jeopardizing their health, the quality of their relationships, career standing, and, in some cases, their sanity. In 1986, in the book *Women's Burnout,* authors Freudenberger and North warned women of the serious physical and psychological damage resulting from trying to do too much.[1] Sylvia Ann Hewlett, author of *A Lesser Life: The Myth of Women's Liberation in America,* confronted the dramatic lack of support systems available to women in this country, saying: "Compared to European women, who enjoy job-protected maternity leave, subsidized childcare, child allowances, lower divorce rates, and a narrowing wage gap, American women have only a precarious security as workers, wives, and mothers."[2]

Article after article, case studies, entire books revealed women cracking under the strain of trying to handle it all. Women like Stacy, a bright, thirty-one-year-old attorney who described the difficult, long years putting herself through school and her delight at being hired as an associate with a large firm specializing in commerce law.

After eighteen months on the job, Stacy became pregnant. During her short maternity leave, her secretary called several times a day with questions. Once, a senior partner sent over, by messenger, a copy of a brief with a scrawled note: "If you get a second, take a look at this and give me a ring."

When she went back to work, Stacy found it increasingly hard to put in the requisite ten-hour days. She tried to keep up with her co-workers, who made no bones about the firm being their absolute priority. She flew from Chicago to Dallas on a half-day's notice. She was sick with bronchitis, running a 103-degree fever, and had to miss her son's first day of nursery school. Stacy recalled sitting in that meeting as if she didn't have a care in the world, pretending everything was just fine.

But it wasn't. Shortly after, Stacy resigned her position, sacrificing the personal satisfaction, stimulation, and substantial salary she had worked so hard for. She saw her decision not as a victory, or even a compromise. In her words: "I quit fighting the system and just gave up."

One article focused on a twenty-eight-year-old woman in Salt Lake City, heartbroken at having to put her three-year-old daughter into full-time childcare so she could go back to work in order to help support her family. An ABC *20/20* special cited the painful quandary of two-career couples raising children in today's world. Several features, including the notorious *Newsweek* cover story of October 10, 1986, "The Marriage Crunch," illustrated the bind of women in their twenties and thirties who, even though successful at their careers, felt cheated and panicky at the poor odds of ever meeting the right person to settle down with and raise a family.

As I took in these articles and specials concerning women struggling to integrate multiple roles, and others of women simply dropping out, I began to wonder if my dilemma wasn't merely a sign of the times. Perhaps, during this unsettling transition from having been raised to follow the traditional role of our mothers to trying to carve out a new one, overwhelming stress and pressure were inevitable. All of my research confirmed that despite the hard-won gains of the women's movement and talk of expanded options and greater equality, without the necessary support systems women were still a long way from "having it all." If anything, we were *doing* it all.

None of which I found particularly comforting. Political and social institutions change over many years through a painstakingly arduous process. The day might come when my daughter could easily shift from one role to another without cost to her health or emotional well-being, but I wasn't about to hold my breath.

I also wasn't about to give up. I wondered if I might have taken a wrong turn, looking to outside factors as the source of my ills. Instead, I decided to direct my attention inward. I asked myself: Why am I feeling like a victim of circumstance, when I normally pride myself on being in charge of my destiny? Could it be that I am in some way contributing to or causing the problem?

I began to see a pattern. There were the times I'd make an extra appointment at work whe.. I was up to my ears in deadlines, or meet a friend for dinner when my house was a mess and then stay up past midnight because I couldn't sleep with dust on the piano. I saw that I was chastising myself for having my children in day-care, whereas their father, who is equally involved with them, went off to work each morning without it seeming to bother him. I saw the way I would take it upon myself to organize family projects, trying to engage everyone in cleaning the den together or wrapping holiday gifts, getting angry when they wouldn't cooperate, and then ending up doing it myself.

Little by little my suspicion grew, from a fuzzy vague feeling to sharp-edged certainty. I was doing something, although I still wasn't sure what, to create *more* pressure in my life than already existed.

But why? Why, at the end of a long productive work day, would anyone in her right mind choose to labor over laundry when there were piles of clean clothes, instead of curling up in front of the television? Why, when I'd gone to the effort to arrange a special night out, did I ruin it by worrying about the kids, the next day's work, or whether I'd remembered to call back the carpet-cleaning service? Why, given the demands already built into my life-style, would I go out of my way to take on more? I knew it wasn't a question of time management or organization. It wasn't even a matter of having more to do than I wanted or could handle. The bigger issue was why I couldn't let go of anything.

I didn't have the answer to my problem. But I sensed I wasn't alone. In 1984, I had founded Expecting Change Workshops, a program offering emotional support to expectant mothers. The workshops were conceived following two difficult pregnancies during which I realized that the importance of pregnancy is greatly downplayed in our society; my own experiences and need for support stirred in me the desire to provide a safe and understanding milieu for women to explore the changes they were experiencing and celebrate the significance of this life-changing event. Through the workshops, I have been privileged to share hundreds of women's experiences. The publication of the book *Expecting Change: The Emotional Journey Through Pregnancy*[3] made it possible to reach many more women.

As we were winding down one evening's workshop, bracing ourselves for the stark blackness and below-zero windchill factor of late February in Minnesota, I turned to the group and tried out my new realization: "I've been thinking how I make myself crazy by pressuring myself to be perfect," I began. And I knew immediately I had struck a chord. One by one, each of the eight women in the room shrugged off her coat and sat back down. Everyone started talking at once. Laura, a twenty-four-year-old graduate student, married just under a year, tried to find words for the constant pounding anxiety that plagued her, particularly when preparing for an exam or an important paper. "I can't stop it," she said. "Nothing helps. I expend three times the energy worrying as I spend doing. I'm depleted before I begin."

"I know just how you feel," interrupted Raleigh, a redhead on leave from her job as a flight attendant. "I'm so wound up, I don't give myself any leeway. When I screw up, even when it's just some dumb little mistake, I'm just a wreck. I don't know why it is, but I know I make things much harder than they have to be." A soft-spoken mother of two talked about never being satisfied with her appearance, sometimes spending as much as three hours in front of the mirror, applying, smudging, removing, and reapplying her makeup. Another woman, thirty-seven years old, who had recently moved to Minneapolis from Boston to head a corporate recruiting firm, shared the conflict she experienced trying to make policy under pressure while worrying about whether she'd remembered to include gummy worms in her five-year-old's lunch.

Joan, a high school teacher who is particularly insightful about her part in creating more pressure, wryly confessed: "I've always applauded myself for being efficient and organized, and secretly prided myself on handling so much. When I went away on vacation, I made fifteen different lists, choreographing intricate babysitting schedules and color-coding the children's outfits." An otherwise quite independent therapist in the group said that even though her husband had to be up for work an hour and a half earlier, she dragged herself out of bed each morning to pour his dry cereal and milk into the bowl, just as her own mother always had for her husband, and then went right back to sleep.

As I listened, I was fascinated with the relationship between the pressure we feel and our need to be perfect. I went on to broaden my inquiry, setting up focus groups with women of all ages, from many walks of life. Was this problem primarily affecting women in their twenties and thirties, trying to live out some version of "Superwoman," or did it reach across generations?

Every woman I spoke with, from the thirty-five-year-old black political activist to the fifty-five-year-old professional volunteer, from the young working mother to the seventy-two-year-old woman who had made her children the center of her life, knew exactly what I meant when I talked about the inner pressure to be perfect.

Despite all the fuss, it was apparent that the media-hyped "New Woman" hadn't cornered the market on stress. Single women, struggling to make it alone, felt no less pressure than those involved in permanent relationships. The stresses of coping with motherhood were no greater than those of trying to do well at work, look good, and keep in shape, while at the same time being the perfect best friend or daughter. Women who identified themselves as liberal or feminists described their feelings of pressure in the same way, and often using the same words, as those more aligned with traditional roles and conservative values.

As hundreds of women shared their feelings—some in the small group settings, others in extensive taped interviews, still others in long personal conversations, sometimes broken in mid-sentence to take a business call or feed a crying infant—certain key phrases were repeatedly spoken: "I'm the only one who can do it," and, "It's all up to me." The theme *"If I don't hold it together, it will all fall apart"* played over and over, until it started to sound like the female battle cry of the eighties.

Across the board, every woman I interviewed spoke of too

much pressure. Yet even as they complained of being overburdened and exhausted, they seemed pleased by their endless catalog of responsibilities, proudly reeling them off like so many titles on a résumé. I had expected that strategies for relieving stress would be appreciated and welcomed. Instead, any suggestions for change were quickly rejected with sarcastic comments like "There's no rest for the wicked," elaborate explanations of situational factors, or long, loud sighs.

"I would have loved to take more time off, but no one at work would begin to know how to do my job," explained a haggard-looking new mother when I asked why she had agreed to a mere three weeks of maternity leave. Another woman, whose opening for her own fabric store coincided with her youngest son's starting elementary school, filled up several notebook pages listing everything she had accomplished the previous day. Every moment was accounted for, with absolutely no leeway for the unexpected and no breathing space built in. That particular day, her alarm clock went off at a quarter to six. Before noon, she had completed the week's bookwork for the store, cleaned the kitchen cupboards, made her children's breakfasts and packed their lunches, arranged the weekend social events, made a deposit at the bank, made dentist appointments for the entire family, held a training session for employees, and called her mother-in-law to wish her a happy birthday.

"Couldn't anything have waited, like the cupboards, for example?" I asked. "Or could some of it have been delegated?"

Her response: "The sitter and the kids baked cookies last night. I couldn't stand the way they left cans of soup mixed up with the flour and baking soda. And as far as asking someone else to do anything—the truth is, by the time I explain how to do something, I've wasted *more* time and energy. It's easier to just do it myself."

I interviewed Lonnie, a woman with a long history of frustrating and difficult romances. She related having recently been sick in bed with an awful cold. Her boyfriend at that time, a rather sweet but passive man named Peter, came over to visit and take care of her, bearing a bouquet of flowers, her favorite magazines, and ingredients for homemade chicken soup, which he proceeded to fix. "There I was, lying in bed with a fever, my face blotchy and red, my nose running, with used Kleenexes all over the floor," said Lonnie. "Do you think I could just lie there and let myself be taken care of? In between sneezing and blowing my nose, I supervised from the bedroom: 'Are you sure you've got the heat on simmer? Have you put in enough salt?' Pretty soon I was up, with my old flannel bathrobe wrapped around me, stirring the soup and serving it to Peter. The whole thing took so much out of me, I collapsed and barely made it back to bed." Gail, the production manager of a direct-mail house and mother of four-year-old twins, tried to understand why a simple oversight left her feeling devastated. "In my mind a perfect mother is always available to her children. If she can't be home, she calls. That's what telephones are for. Because this is my image, and because we are the parents of two young children and we go out fairly often, I long ago promised myself to always call home and say good-night before the kids went to sleep.

"I never broke my word until one night last winter when my husband and I were out buying holiday presents. Suddenly, while standing in the checkout line, I spotted a clock. It was *ten* and I was an hour late. You'd have thought I'd committed a crime! I rushed to a phone, dialed home, and without trying to disguise the panic in my voice, asked the babysitter whether the kids were asleep. They were. 'Wake them up!' I insisted, certain that my sleeping children couldn't sleep unless their mother said good-night."

As I listened to these and similar stories, my thoughts returned to Stacy, the Chicago attorney. Her predicament took on a new light, as I questioned why she had been so quick to allow herself to be intimidated and, ultimately, beaten down by her colleagues' expectations. I wondered how much of her pressure was really coming from the firm and how much from herself. I began to understand the feelings of pressure *and* pride inherent in being the one who can handle everything, and the *only* one who can, the one who can always be counted on to be there, no matter what.

Although the individual stories were unique, they had one important thing in common. Each and every woman was compounding her own pressure by making herself indispensable. It was clear that regardless of how much we bemoaned the pressure, we were reluctant to let it go. Because *having* it reassures us we are wanted and needed.

HOW MUCH IS ENOUGH

The first step toward change is identifying how you are making yourself indispensable.

The *Oxford English Dictionary* defines someone who is *indispensable* as a person who *can't be done without or set aside;* one who is *absolutely necessary.*

How do you know if you are making yourself indispensable? To reveal your personal attitudes, beliefs, and behaviors, answer YES or NO to the following questions:

1. Do you typically take on more than you can *comfortably* handle?

2. Does the idea that you can give up any of your responsibilities strike you as ridiculous?

3. Is it hard for you to ask for and accept help and support?

4. Are you typically rushing and late for appointments?

5. Is your life fragmented and overcompartmentalized?

6. Do you secretly believe that no one can do it as well, as fast, or as efficiently as you?

7. Do tight deadlines and extra responsibility make you feel challenged and exhilarated?

8. Do you hide your insecurities behind a veil of overcompetence?

9. Do you believe that other people don't appreciate how hard you work and how much you do?

10. Do feelings of accomplishment in one part of your life *not* necessarily carry over into another?

11. Do you get so wrapped up in a project, you lose sight of what else is happening around you?

12. Are you extremely goal-oriented?

13. Do you find yourself resenting how much responsibility you have and wondering how you got it?

14. Are you chronically tense, frazzled, and exhausted?

15. Is it hard for you to relax and enjoy yourself, because you're worrying about what *isn't* being done?

16. Is there a gap between what you *are* responsible for and what you *feel* responsible for?

17. Do you experience a constant need to prove yourself?

18. When your demands pile up, do you snap

into action and come up with more efficient and organized means of handling them?

19. Do you find it difficult to sit still and do nothing?

20. Do you feel your best isn't enough?

If you answered YES to more than five of these questions, you are in some stage of becoming or being an Indispensable Woman. Some aspects of the definition may seem unfamiliar while others fit like a glove. You may relate wholeheartedly to some, and less so to others.

RECOGNIZING THE PATTERN

Like most behavioral patterns, making yourself indispensable doesn't happen overnight. Rather, gradually, over a long course of time, you have established relationships in which you assume more than your share of responsibility, and thereby gain acceptance, approval, and love.

Most women start out with the best of intentions. They put a lot of effort into their work, their relationships, their children, because they care. The woman who cares about having an immaculate home, who is the perennial volunteer, who devotes herself to her lover, or who vows always to be home when her children come off the school bus is motivated by feelings of love and commitment. It is when that love becomes a desire to control, when that commitment turns into an unrelenting need to prove her worth, that she is in trouble.

For example, when you first begin a job, it's natural to want to work hard and impress your co-workers and boss. But when no amount of effort feels sufficient and you are driven to perform and perform and perform, then you have crossed the line into seeking indispensability. In the same vein, what starts out as an intensely involved love relationship can turn into controlling obsessiveness. Or, the most genuine desire to help your children succeed can get twisted until you are being pushy, trying to dominate, or even forgetting they are persons in their own right with their own lives to live.

But in the beginning, we are motivated by our needs. We *all* need to be needed. Knowing that we play a significant role and make a valuable contribution is part of what makes us believe we matter.

I first met Marta when she was my academic adviser during my junior year at the university. A large-boned woman of Scandinavian descent, Marta was the sort of person others naturally gravitated toward. She was warm, with a quick, easy smile, and appeared to have unlimited energy for dealing with people's problems. Our time together often ran over the allotted forty-five minutes, the topics moving freely from whether I could fit Abnormal Psych into my schedule to her helping me sort out feelings about my boyfriend.

Marta's dedication to her students went beyond the norm. Many of us wondered how she was able to give so much. We knew there was more to her life; on her desk were pictures of her husband and teenaged children. On several occasions, I noticed her office light late at night on my way home from cramming at the library. If a student needed her help, she always made time.

After I graduated, I stayed in touch with Marta until she moved to San Francisco to get her master's in counseling. Six years later I contacted her when I was in California on business.

Although her children were grown and her husband, Steven, had taken early retirement, her life-style had changed very little. Upon completing her degree, she started a job in a counseling agency where she often worked fifty hours a week. Though she was a relative newcomer to the area, she had cultivated a circle of friends who depended on her for support.

When Marta first bounded into the restaurant, she seemed

filled with her usual buoyancy and good cheer. But as we talked, the corners of her mouth and her shoulders began to droop. Her exhaustion showed as she told me how tired she had become of feeling pulled in so many directions, everyone wanting a piece of her. She self-consciously mentioned the twenty pounds she'd gained, the result of compulsive eating and lethargy.

Marta tried to make sense of her feelings: "I used to be such a patient person," she began, "but lately I have such a short fuse! I practically have to force myself to pay attention when people speak, and I get so irritated with hearing about all their problems." She went on to say, "I feel cheated out of time with Steven, but I'm afraid if I turn down a client or say no to facilitating an extra group, they'll think I'm not serious. And if work wasn't enough, my so-called friends are beginning to feel like part of my caseload. No one even thinks to ask how *I'm* doing. There just isn't anything left over for me."

For Marta, a genuine desire to be there for others had turned into a nightmare of incessant demands. Instead of balancing her needs with those of the people around her, she had promoted herself as someone who could always be depended on. Her perfectionism had backfired. What before had felt flattering and secure, now felt like a trap.

Marta needed to cut back her hours at work, and, more importantly, to learn to say no. Later chapters focus on specific strategies for how to stop putting out more than is realistic.

Historically, we women have been conditioned to see ourselves as care-givers and nurturers; our self-esteem is largely based on our ability to relate to and provide for others. Even as we become more independent, we still continue to put other people's needs ahead of our own.

Making ourselves indispensable goes way beyond wanting to be needed. Our unconscious goal is to be so desirable, so smart, so competent, so giving, so perfect, that others will be convinced they can't get along as well, if at all, without us. In our effort to guarantee career security and advancement, to hold on to our relationships, and, mostly, to create and maintain a positive image of ourselves, we pretend we are infallible and that nothing is beyond our scope.

In a society that judges self-worth on productivity, it's no wonder we fall prey to the misconception that the more we do, the more we're worth. Adding to the pressure, today our self-esteem is based on achievement in many avenues of life. Whether in the privacy of our homes or in the demanding milieu of the workplace, in our primary relationships with our lovers, children, parents, co-workers, or friends, we approach life as if it were an assignment, with a good report card the reward.

At work, particularly for those of us in competitive, high-pressure settings, it's understandably difficult to trust that we will be accepted and appreciated for who we are, rather than on the basis of our productivity. Even so, we are prone to overlay expectations of perfection on top of the already existing standards, pushing ourselves to prove our worth indisputably so that we feel more secure in our positions. And we transfer the same standard into other areas of our lives, pressuring ourselves to have well-conditioned bodies, beautifully kept homes, and fluency in our love-making and interpersonal skills. Instead of accepting that our best is enough, nothing less than perfection reassures us that we have a place and that we are valued.

THE PERFECTION TRAP

Perfection is an illusion and an impossible goal. We all know that no one is perfect. Yet who doesn't have an image of the perfect mother, infallible friend, ideal partner, or ultimate professional? Our idea of perfection is created out of the conglomeration of positive images we've internalized from birth. The most vivid role model, by far, is our parents, particularly our mothers. Even though, as we grow up, our blind adoration of her is tempered by an awareness of her limitations, and in some cases, by grave disappointment, our earliest images are deeply imbedded. In her book, *The Crisis of the Working Mother,* author Barbara J. Berg says, "Experts believe that there is probably no other role with less latitude than our idea of the perfect mother. Firmly fixed in our young minds, our mothers' ways became our ideal."[4]

Our image of perfection is highly personal and varies according to the primary influences that shaped our upbringing. One person may have internalized the ideal of the "good woman," gracious, accommodating, eternally sacrificing her needs to make other people's lives more comfortable. Another woman may make a 180-degree turn, rejecting the traditional model exemplified by her mother. For her, female perfection may be wrapped up in attaining independence and acquiring worldly success. I had the relatively unusual experience, for a woman my age, of having a mother who had a full-time career. As a newspaper reporter, her job was demanding, involving long hours away from home; yet somehow, she managed always to be on hand when I needed her. As a full-time mother and writer, I expect no less of myself, and I am often disappointed.

Many women today, whose chosen life-style is a major departure from that of their mothers, are trying to emulate both their parents. They strive to fulfill their idea of the perfect mother *and* father, expecting themselves to create a home and maintain warm, personal relationships while simultaneously developing careers and making their mark.

Here, two and two adds up to more than four. Trying to integrate the tough, aggressive male model with the passive nurturer most of us were groomed to be creates inner conflict and added pressure. It is precisely this conflict that causes one woman, intent on proving her commitment, to be defensive and apologetic when she must miss work to care for her sick child. The same conflict creates crippling self-doubt in the single woman, successful at her career, yet convinced she is lacking for not having fulfilled more traditional expectations. Another woman, for fear of being a negligent mother and denying her children their rightful time with her, remains at home, despite intense yearnings to express her creativity in a more worldly arena.

Trying to live up to an ideal is dangerous, whether it's the "good woman" and protective care-giver, the consummate provider, or the best of both mother and father rolled into one. When you measure yourself against these images, believing in them as reachable goals, you set yourself up for frustration in two ways.

First, since perfection is unattainable, even your best efforts result in feelings of disappointment and self-defeat. Instead of seeing that it is your ideal, *not* your behavior, that is flawed, you blame and castigate yourself, like Gail, when she forgot to call home at exactly nine o'clock. Rather than reexamining and altering your expectations, you push yourself harder, looking for ways to speed up or improve your performance.

Second, you set yourself up by encouraging others to have Herculean expectations of you. You prove your indispensability by:

• **Making yourself overly available and accessible.**

This is different from being willing to make time for other people or being responsible to their needs. The key word is "overly," meaning you are physically or emotionally present regardless of whether you have the time, energy, or inclination.

• **Chronically putting your needs on hold or diminishing their importance.**

By consistently acting stoically and self-sacrificing, you convince others they needn't take care of you.

• **Promoting an image of yourself as infallible. No mistakes allowed!**

Everyone occasionally falters. The Indispensable Woman can't risk the appearance of hesitation or uncertainty.

• Taking responsibility for other people's problems and trying to fix them.

It can be confusing to discern between *taking an interest* and *taking over,* between making ourselves useful and making ourselves indispensable.

• Promising results beyond what is realistic.

Setting responsible goals means accepting limitations. Heroism pretends there aren't any.

The more you do, the more everyone expects. And the more you expect of yourself. You set the tone. At first, you second-guess other people's expectations, imagining you *must* perform, regardless of what messages they are actually conveying. Before long, what's imagined becomes real. After a while, your employer, friends, and family tailor their expectations to match your image of yourself, happily agreeing to your persistent offers of help. Even those closest to you take your apparent lack of vulnerability at face value and stop extending their support.

Once you've established your indispensability, you pressure yourself to maintain it—a pattern you can learn to undo. Women who have made themselves central in other people's lives work hard in order to stay there. Their fear of losing ground, losing face, losing love, losing hard-won identity propels them to push harder and harder. Anything short of perfection—acknowledging limitations or asking for help—might be misconstrued as weakness, a risk the Indispensable Woman can't afford if she is to remain irreplaceable.

HIGH STRESS/
LOW SELF-ESTEEM

▼

Physicians, psychotherapists, counselors, and other professionals working in the health-care industry have identified the physical and emotional symptoms of stress. The women I interviewed described the feelings of stress generated by perfectionism in three typical ways: "as an overwhelming preoccupation with infinite details," "like an internal time bomb ticking away inside my head," and as if "someone is standing over me, wielding a whip, grimly urging me on."

In the early stages of making yourself indispensable, you are unlikely to be aware of any of these feelings. You've probably experienced the sensation of having too many things going on at the same time. At first, there is a sense of exhilaration; your adrenaline races with the drama of trying to coordinate it all. After a while, you begin to fade; you feel anxious, ragged. Finally, when it all somehow gets done, you're simply glad it's over. Or as one woman put it: "I never know I have too many plates spinning until I'm breathlessly trying to keep them in place, one slips out, and they all come crashing down around me."

Having too much responsibility initially creates feelings of self-importance. But for Susan, a twenty-eight-year-old executive, the pressure began to take over.

There was no such thing as spare time in Susan's family while she was growing up. When Susan's mother caught her daydreaming, she'd set up an art project or ask her to help around the house. During high school, Susan was an "A" student, a cheerleader, a member of the track team, and president of the senior class. She graduated college with honors, picked up an MBA, and, at twenty-eight, accepted a vice presidency with a prestigious advertising agency.

On the surface, it looked as if Susan had everything. She was smart, pretty, and accomplished. Inside, she was starting to fall apart.

When I first interviewed Susan, she had been at the agency only two weeks. She told me how excited she was to be on a team with other professionals and supervising a management staff of three. Her outward appearance crackled with authority, but the one time we sat down together over lunch, she quietly confided her doubts: "This is the first really important job I've ever had. Do you think I can pull it off?"

If the truth be known, Susan was in a little over her head. In order to keep up, she took work home in the evenings and set her alarm for five, which gave her an extra hour and a half in the morning to prepare. Although her performance was up to par for her experience, it didn't nearly equal her expectations. If something came up she didn't understand, she'd fudge, pretending to have the answer. Instead of asking for guidance from her more seasoned peers, she went out of her way to act as if she was in a position to help *them*.

As a senior executive, Susan participated in weekly briefings. The first week, she offered to be in charge of a research focus group. Within a month, she volunteered to head another committee and agreed to edit the agency newsletter. Soon, Susan had a list of extra projects over and above her regular work load. With so much to look out for, she monopolized meetings. And, to the increasing embarrassment of her boss, others began having trouble getting a word in edgewise.

The same thing occurred at the biweekly section meetings. Susan, who considered herself a natural leader, automatically took over. When the group needed a spokesperson, she nominated herself. When there were loose ends on a project, Susan off-handedly suggested members of the group go on ahead—she'd finish it up herself. No matter how efficiently Susan worked, it seemed she never managed to finish at six o'clock like the rest of the staff.

Rick, her husband of less than two years, began to complain of Susan's absence. He resented having dinner alone, missed her companionship, and accused her of becoming a workaholic. For the first time in their marriage, they had serious differences. Rick insinuated Susan's career was more important to her than their relationship. Susan bitterly denied it, insisting she was just doing what was expected. She reminded him that on those evenings she worked late, she prepared dinner ahead of time, and even though she was exhausted, she still found the energy to visit with him and straighten up the house.

"I could manage everything fine if you'd just leave me alone," screamed Susan in frustration in the middle of one of their arguments.

"Manage? You can barely manage to comb your hair anymore!" Rick angrily exploded. "Have you noticed the way you've been looking lately? You're so busy being a one-woman show at the office, you've stopped caring about anything else. And do you suppose we might make love sometime? Or should I call your secretary for an appointment?"

Susan stormed out of the house and drove to a nearby park. No one, least of all Rick, understood her. Why didn't anyone give her credit when she was trying so hard? All she wanted was to do her best. But instead of appreciating her, Rick blamed her for their problems, and at work, no one seemed to notice her efforts. The more she did, the less impressed her boss appeared to be, and just two days earlier, her administrative assistant had left in a huff when Susan was merely trying to show her a better way to write the proposal.

Over the next few months, Susan became more and more isolated. She and Rick politely co-existed, mostly in stony silence, occasionally broken by brief conversational overtures. Susan spent even more time at the office, trying to lose herself in work. But she felt equally alienated there; although her co-workers grudgingly admired her productivity, they rarely spoke to her, except on matters of business. She had refused lunch invitations so many times in the past, gulping down a sandwich at her desk so she could get more done, that she was no longer invited. Once, when she was rushing toward an especially tight deadline, she lost her temper after her assistant, Kate, made an error that had to be corrected. "Can't you even type without making a mistake?" Susan said. The minute the words were out of her mouth she regretted them. "I'm sorry," said Susan, tears filling her eyes. "I just don't know what's wrong with me anymore." Kate hesitantly moved closer, saying, "We've all been worried about you. Is there anything I can do?" A warm flush spread across Susan's face. She suddenly became very involved in straightening her desk and briskly replied, "I'm fine. Whatever would give you the idea there's anything wrong?"

Susan was so deeply invested in looking as if she had it all together, she couldn't see the physical and emotional toll exacted by her drive to be indispensable. She began having stomach pains. She first noticed them during an especially heavy period, and assumed they would pass. But they steadily worsened, and though she tried to ignore them and didn't tell Rick, he found out when twice after eating she became violently ill. Rick insisted she go to the doctor, but she refused, cynically remarking, "I'm sure it's just stress—one of the occupational hazards of success." But as her health deteriorated, Susan's work suffered. Because of the frequent pain, she was having trouble sleeping at night, which affected her concentration. In order to compensate for being less effective, Susan worked even longer hours than before, drinking coffee all day to curb her hunger and grabbing Tums and a donut before bed.

Around this time, Rick's father became very ill. A severe stroke left him paralyzed and unable to communicate. Rick took a leave and flew to Seattle to be with him for two weeks. While he respected his father, Rick had always found him stiff and unapproachable. But now, perhaps for the first time, Rick was able to let himself feel how much he loved and needed him. And, during his and Susan's hiatus, Rick spent much time thinking about their marriage.

When he returned, their first night home together, Rick once again asked Susan to see a doctor, but this time he offered to go with her. Susan agreed. After extensive tests, she discovered her stomach pain was caused by an ulcer. Her doctor advised her of the seriousness of her condition and recommended slowing down and making dietary changes. Sensing her tension level, he also gently urged her to seek professional help for herself and for her marriage.

OVERCOMING
DENIAL

It is very difficult to see ourselves clearly when we are in the midst of making ourselves sick. In Susan's case, it took the disintegration of her marriage, difficulties at work, and illness for her to stop and reevaluate her life. Over time she was able to acknowledge her vulnerabilities, let down, and let others, including Rick, nurture and support her.

The Indispensable Woman holds tightly to an image of herself as supercharged and successful, even when she doesn't feel that way at all. Because she responds to problems by snapping into action, signs of fatigue or conflict are seen as a challenge, or even something to boast or joke about, rather than red flags to slow down and retrench. Inside, she may secretly wish a blizzard would close down shop, giving her time to catch up. She nurses a fantasy of escaping into a desert island, where no one, *no one* expects anything of her. But to the world, she looks as if she expects to be named "Woman of the Year." She pretends things are other than they are, because it is too frightening or painful to face reality.

Denial also operates by reinforcing an image of ourselves as victims of extenuating circumstances, blinding us to our own responsibility for what happens in our lives. Rather than seeing how *we* create more pressure by making ourselves indispensable, we attribute the stress to being a high achiever, having too much responsibility, or both.

Many women have extremely busy, heavily structured lives, with only minimal opportunity for rest and relaxation. Consequently, feeling indispensable is often confused with and incorrectly traced to having too much to do, when, in fact, that is only a small part of the problem. The complex responsibilities you face each day may seem like the direct source of your pressure. But juggling multiple roles doesn't cause the problem, it merely exacerbates it.

When asked why their life-styles are so fraught with stress, the vast majority of women reply with some version of: "That's what it takes to succeed." Looking at female ambitiousness and drive, particularly through the prism of the hard-won gains of the women's movement, it is easy enough to understand the fear of doing less or letting down even a little. For most of us, the only model of achievement, which is a male model, rests on the ability to focus on an end product, commit all your resources, and race toward the finish line in the hope of claiming victory.

But making yourself indispensable is qualitatively different from doing your best or "going for it." The pursuit of excellence comes from the desire for self-fulfillment, career advancement, status, or wealth. It is based on the desire to stretch your capabilities so as to fulfill your potential, *not* on the search for perfection.

The following chart illustrates the contrast between striving to excel and making yourself indispensable:

High Achievement	Indispensability
Is deliberately pursued.	Is compulsive.
Involves prioritizing, reasonable goal-setting, and compromise.	Knows no limits.
Requires the willingness and courage to take risks.	Attempts to control every outcome.
Occurs situationally, in response to specific challenges.	Develops gradually and systematically, worsening over time.
Provides deep, satisfying rewards.	Results in physical decline and emotional drain.

WHEN BEING EVERYWHERE AT ONCE LEAVES YOU NOWHERE

▼

There's nothing wrong with having a great deal of responsibility or wanting to be the very best person you are capable of being. Both are part of a full, satisfying life, and while they may contribute to your overall level of stress, neither will cause serious damage to your emotional or physical health. In fact, some researchers have found that having many and multifaceted responsibilities can enhance a woman's overall well-being.[5]

Conversely, making yourself indispensable, as you will see in the many personal stories shared by women throughout this book, warrants serious cause for concern. It is a self-destructive pattern that at first appears to increase productivity, but eventually erodes our energy and ability to cope. Over time, the physical products of indispensability include exhaustion, reduced immunity, illness, and, ultimately, potential collapse. The emotional repercussions include anxiety, alienation, and depression, resulting in major life-crises, such as career trauma and divorce.

A primary purpose of this book is to clarify the difference between healthy productivity that results in enhanced self-esteem and the pattern of indispensability that inevitably destroys it. You will be shown ways of lessening pressure without radically altering your life-style. The object isn't to give up doing what gives you satisfaction. Rather, you will learn how to let go of the inner pressure that inhibits fulfillment of your goals, ambitions, and dreams.

Change is possible and well within reach. If you can slow down long enough to acknowledge the areas of your life where you are making yourself indispensable, then you can begin to make necessary and important strides. Awareness is the first step. The process of recovery includes naming the problem and finding alternative paths.

TWO

CHARACTERISTICS OF THE INDISPENSABLE WOMAN

You may be running too fast to recognize how you resemble the Indispensable Woman. If you think you're too busy, that it's out of the question to stop and take inventory, then *now's* the time.

It's natural to blame feelings of pressure on situational factors or an inability to manage stress, but too often these justifications only serve to keep us stuck. It's necessary to move beyond excuses and even good reasons, in order to allow yourself to see how you may be making yourself indispensable. *Creating more pressure than actually exists* is one of the hallmarks of the Indispensable Woman.

Since you probably feel as if the pressure in your life is inevitable, it's tricky to see how you are complicit in its creation. This quiz can help determine your Personal Pressure Quotient. Choose the one answer that most closely applies.

1. I usually feel as if . . .
    a. there is plenty of time to accomplish everything
    b. with a little more time, I could get everything done
    c. I am trying to catch up
    d. No matter how hard I try, it will never all get done

2. If something unexpected comes up . . .
    a. I do my best to move things around and fit it into my schedule
    b. I deal with it only if it's really important
    c. I feel guilty unless I say yes
    d. I always come through

3. My friends can depend on me to . . .
    a. put them first some of the time
    b. be there unless there's something absolutely pressing
    c. drop everything
    d. be honest about my limitations

4. When there's too much expected of me I feel . . .
    a. overwhelmed
    b. resentful
    c. exhilarated
    d. challenged

5. If I went away for a month, the closest people in my life would . . .
    a. be fine
    b. reluctantly adjust
    c. find it more difficult to function
    d. fall apart

6. When I complete a project, I usually feel . . .
   a. let down
   b. relieved
   c. sure that if I had more time, I'd get it right
   d. satisfied

7. When others offer their help or support . . .
   a. I gratefully accept
   b. I find it easier to do it myself
   c. I consider it an affront
   d. I sometimes accept, depending on the circumstances

8. I feel important . . .
   a. all of the time
   b. most of the time
   c. some of the time
   d. rarely, if ever

9. I know that I'm doing a good job . . .
   a. because others say so
   b. if I've tried hard
   c. by the quality of the outcome
   d. when there's nothing left to be done

10. When I excel in one area of my life . . .
    a. I take pleasure in my success
    b. I look for another challenge
    c. I am briefly content
    d. I worry about being able to repeat it

11. Members of my family . . .
    a. can't understand why I feel so pressured
    b. remark on how well I cope
    c. tell me to slow down
    d. don't appreciate me

12. If all my responsibilities magically disap-
    peared, I'd . . .
    a. rebuild a simpler life
    b. feel empty
    c. drift aimlessly
    d. replace them as soon as possible

SCORING

Give yourself the following points for your answers:

1. a. 4	b. 6	c. 8	d. 10
2. a. 6	b. 4	c. 8	d. 10
3. a. 8	b. 6	c. 10	d. 4
4. a. 6	b. 4	c. 10	d. 8
5. a. 4	b. 6	c. 8	d. 10
6. a. 10	b. 6	c. 8	d. 4
7. a. 4	b. 10	c. 8	d. 6
8. a. 10	b. 8	c. 6	d. 4
9. a. 8	b. 6	c. 4	d. 10
10. a. 4	b. 6	c. 10	d. 8
11. a. 6	b. 10	c. 4	d. 8
12. a. 4	b. 8	c. 10	d. 6

48-65 points

You strike a healthy balance between doing enough and doing too
much. There is plenty of pressure in your life, but your priorities
are straight, and although you may hesitate, you're quite capable
of saying no. Feeling needed flatters you, but doesn't keep you
from taking care of yourself. You accept your limitations and know
that doing your best is enough.

66-84 points

At this point, you still maintain a fairly realistic picture of what you can handle. Nevertheless, although you try, you're never completely satisfied with yourself. You brush off compliments and worry about whether your relationships are secure. If you have a career, you do more than the job description requires. Although you are working at putting yourself first, doing so feels like a risk.

85-102 points

You feel guilty when you say no, the people in your life depend on you too much, and your commitments are beginning to be more than you bargained for. You've always been a high achiever, but lately it seems as if there's no way off the treadmill. You'd like to have more time for yourself, but you can't figure out what to give up.

103-120 points

An image of perfection is the mirror against which you measure yourself. Since it's impossible to live up to perfection, you are continually caught in a trap of trying to exceed your limitations.

Perfectionism has many faces. You may recognize aspects of your behavior in one of the following types:

THE VACUUM automatically sweeps up whatever is in her path. Her work load expands to include whatever isn't being taken care of. Uncomfortable with anything left undone, THE VACUUM does everything herself.

If there isn't any work to do, *poof!*, THE MAGICIAN makes herself indispensable by creating more. No projects? No problem, THE MAGICIAN cooks some up. Then, she gets them taken care of.

"I'll do it for less" is THE DISCOUNT's motto. She makes herself indispensable by coming through without expecting appreciation or attention in return. Her time, services, and even love are less expensive, so they're in great demand.

If there's a job to be done, THE VOLUNTEER makes herself indispensable by offering to pick up the slack. In order to maintain a positive image of herself, she makes herself available, accessible, and often exhausted.

THE EXPERT has the right answer, the perfect solution, and the best way to handle everything. Since she knows it all, she feels obligated to *do* it all.

You may relate in part to some or even all these types. While each reveals a different way in which perfectionism is manifested, all are ways of taking on more responsibility than is actually warranted.

Cari, a thirty-one-year-old assistant buyer for a large department store, shared her feelings of pressure shortly after seeking counseling for marital problems. When Cari and Alex met, he was a struggling musician. She aspired to be a professional dancer. Although they were talented and dedicated, neither was able to make enough of a living. They held part-time jobs on the side, but still couldn't make ends meet.

When Cari first applied for the buyer training program, Alex teased her about selling out and working for the establishment. Although she felt defensive, she kept her feelings to herself. Alex pursued his music career, often playing late-night gigs and sleeping until noon. Cari managed day-to-day arrangements and all their financial and social obligations. Although Alex made good money off and on, hers was the only steady income.

In the meantime, Cari's dance career was going downhill. Classes were held at inconvenient times and rehearsals conflicted with her work schedule. Although she had exhibited tremendous potential, she could now barely muster the energy to flex a toe.

At times, Cari resented Alex's erratic life-style and freedom to come and go as he pleased. She questioned why she was doing so much of the work. When she proposed they split regular tasks, he said everything was always done before he had a chance to get to it. She mentioned that he could at least fold the laundry and wash the dishes, to which he angrily replied, "Are you kidding, all I'd get is a lecture on how to do it *right*. Although I suppose now you're making the bucks, I'd better get busy learning how to be a wife!"

One night, Cari was asked to go out for a drink after work with a few of the other buyers. It was the first time she had been included and she called to tell Alex she'd be home late. He seemed disgruntled when she reminded him to finish addressing the invitations for their New Year's party and said she'd appreciate his taking out the garbage before he went to bed.

When Cari quietly let herself in at one A.M., Alex was fast asleep. She could smell the stench from the hallway, and while the invitations were addressed, none of them had zip codes or stamps. Furious, Cari stomped around the apartment collecting the garbage until she saw Alex watching from the bedroom doorway. "Can't you ever quit?" he demanded. "I'm sick of how everything around here has to be done to your specifications. I can't do a goddamn thing right."

Cari was stunned. She had assumed that in order to be a good person and a good wife, she needed to hold everything together. She hadn't even known she was angry. When Alex didn't help, she made excuses, telling herself he needed to conserve his creative energy. It hadn't occurred to Cari that her perfectionism was making it harder for Alex to participate; for fear of not living up to her standards, he was slowly abdicating his share of the work and moving emotionally away from the relationship. Cari's alternating bossiness and silent heroics were a way of punishing Alex for his lack of involvement. He retaliated by acting like a sullen child instead of taking responsibility for his part. Through it all, Cari maintained (and genuinely believed) that everything she did was in Alex's best interests.

MISGUIDED
MOTIVES
▼

Like Cari, many of us experience confusion between genuinely wanting to give and giving because we want something back.

It was important for Cari to learn the difference in order to see that she had a stake in Alex's doing less than his share. That in fact, she had become a martyr, giving and giving, not from her heart, but grudgingly and with resentment. It is perfectly human to give because we want to be needed, appreciated, and loved. Think of the times you agree to do some task without having the appropriate knowledge or expertise simply because you want to be thought of as competent. Or someone needs a favor and you volunteer without considering prior obligations so as to enhance that person's impression of you. Or your mate, mother, or a friend is having problems and you leap to the rescue in order to "save" them. It's not that you're intentionally deceptive, just unable to see how you are meeting your *own* needs, even though others may benefit in the process.

What gets us in trouble is when we are blind or dishonest about our motivations. As we pretend to ourselves, our perception of reality becomes increasingly distorted. Like the small child who insists she can stay up way past midnight, with eyes glazed, head propped rigidly against the pillow, straining to keep awake, we promote an image that is neither real nor possible to maintain.

Dishonesty implies a deliberate attempt to conceal the truth. But for the Indispensable Woman, the line is blurred between dishonesty and lack of awareness. Because you aren't conscious of your motivations, it's difficult to change your behavior.

Long-term change demands the courage and willingness to explore feelings, a subject which will be explored in depth later in this book. Acknowledging feelings can be frightening, especially if you are accustomed to presenting an impenetrable facade to the world. Looking at yourself in terms of behavioral characteristics is a less threatening, important first step toward building awareness.

Following are the eight most common characteristics of how the Indispensable Woman operates:

1. Overcommitment

2. Fragmentation

3. Tunnel vision

4. Nontransferable credits

5. Self-effacement/grandiosity

6. The need to prove yourself

7. Co-dependence

8. Inability to ask for or accept support

As you read through the description of each characteristic, consider how it is similar to your experience. Notice ways in which the patterns resemble your own.

OVERCOMMITMENT

There are only twenty-four hours in a day, but the Indispensable Woman tries to squeeze in more. Like the airlines, she schedules appointments when she's already overbooked. Consequently she's impatient, often in the position of having to apologize, and almost always running behind.

While at first glance being overextended seems aggravating and exhausting, it has several things to recommend it. For starters, it appeals to your sense of urgency and drama. And having a tight schedule makes you seem more important and forces others to accommodate your itinerary and compete for your time.

Living life at a frenetic pace precludes the peace and solitude necessary to respond to inner feelings, which sooner or later leads to serious problems. Consider what happened to Dana as she became more and more overcommitted.

My first impression of her, as Dana and I settled into her comfortable den for our interview, was of someone who had come to terms with herself—which she had, but only very recently. A mere two months before she had been ready to throw in the towel.

Dana was overjoyed when her promotion to divisional manager was announced. After six years of working her way up the ladder at the bank, she felt deserving of the title and the raise. But once Dana was actually in the position, the pressures began to mount. While before her job had been relatively undemanding, she now took work home regularly, often burning the candle at both ends.

Since being divorced, Dana had also given her social life high priority. She dated a lot and her home was a frequent gathering place for friends. A season ticket holder to the chamber orchestra and repertory theater, she kept her calendar nicely filled out.

In her new position, besides keeping up with several major new clients and an increased managerial work load, she was expected to develop community networks. When asked to chair a chamber of commerce committee, she felt obliged to accept. As a way of building positive public relations, she was also expected to entertain for dinner at least twice a week.

After three months of her whirlwind schedule, the strain began to show. No longer able to put her feet up and wrap herself around a good novel, Dana usually dragged herself into bed. Many evenings were spent brushing up for the next day's meeting; one man she had been particularly interested in stopped calling. The headaches that had virtually disappeared since college came back, and several times Dana woke in the middle of the night with anxiety attacks, was unable to fall back asleep, and spent restless hours half dreaming her way through endless appointments, presentations, and business banquets.

The bottom fell out one awful Monday morning when Dana

was called to the vice president's office. There, she was informed that a mistake had been made in her department to the tune of several thousand dollars. Head spinning, Dana felt her face turn beet red. "It can't be," she said, looking for a way out, but in the pit of her stomach, she knew it was true.

After much soul-searching and talking with her supervisor, who was extremely sensitive, Dana decided to take a month's leave of absence. During that time, she slept, took long walks, and thought about what really mattered. She vowed never again to let her job take over her life. Once she returned to work, she scaled back her responsibilities and hired an assistant, two important steps toward repairing her indispensability.

We become overcommitted when we are out of touch with our limitations. Fortunately, Dana had the insight and support to make significant changes before too much damage was done. There are times when unusual circumstances dictate the need to increase responsibilities—family emergencies, uncommon work pressures, or a crowded holiday schedule—but for the Indispensable Woman, being overextended is a way of life. When faced with the choice of cutting back or accelerating, she inevitably pushes down the gas pedal.

Being overextended keeps you so busy *doing* that you have little time to *feel*. The rush of perpetual motion creates an illusion of purpose, but in truth, you barely have time to get where you're going, much less know if it's the right place to be.

FRAGMENTATION

Your life as an Indispensable Woman is compartmentalized. In order to keep the various little boxes in working order, your days must be terribly structured and organized. You live by a list, with each moment accounted for. When something goes wrong or the unexpected occurs, it becomes nearly impossible to keep things straight. There is little, if any, room for error, as Jeanine, a high-strung twenty-eight-year-old lobbyist found out.

"I'm falling apart" were her first words when Jeanine called frantically to ask her husband to come quickly and transport her to where her car had been towed. As they drove, she explained to him what had happened, her words spilling out like a waterfall.

"Things got totally behind at the office and I was rushing so I wouldn't be late to pick Barry up at school," she started. "I got out to the car and realized I had forgotten my briefcase, so I had to go back in and get it. By then, I knew I'd be late, so I phoned the school, and then as I was running out my boss stopped me in the hall to ask about some work for tomorrow. I swear I was rude to him, I think I cut him off, but I was rushing so, worrying about work and Barry, and by the time I got outside the *car* was gone! It had been towed away. I couldn't believe it! I was so nervous about this morning's committee testimony and our anniversary party tonight, that I left my checkbook at home this morning so I had no money to get the car back. I ended up calling my mother to pick up Barry and needing you to bail me out."

Jeanine is actually a very organized person, which made it all the more frustrating for her to be in this kind of fix. For her life to run smoothly, each aspect of her identity needed to be synchronized, like so many tiny parts inside a watch.

It's hard to have a peaceful sense of yourself as a whole, integrated person when you're split into so many pieces. No one part of your life is truly on track. Women who are fragmented say that at best, they are in a constant state of anxiety; at worst, they feel as if they are on the verge of a nervous breakdown.

TUNNEL VISION

Tunnel vision skews your perception so that you only see what's directly in front of you. The Indispensable Woman puts on blinders, concentrating intensely on the task at hand, to the exclusion of all else.

Some women describe being so overly focused on their children, they lose sight of their need for romantic time with their mates. Or being so obsessed with a relationship, they aren't productive at work. Or so preoccupied at work, they can't enjoy themselves on the weekend.

Fear usually underlies tunnel vision. You may worry that if you relax your grip or take your eye off the focal point, you won't be able to perform or finish a task. Ironically, your productivity is hampered by losing your perspective. You'd be amazed at how often a short respite encourages rather than distracts the process.

Tunnel vision is a coping mechanism, a way to handle competing mental and emotional demands. However, being overly focused can turn into being fixated, preventing you from fully experiencing your life in the present.

Remember the fabric-store owner whose kitchen cupboards just couldn't wait? She discussed her tunnel vision, saying: "I am often so absorbed in work that when a friend calls or my mother invites me to lunch, even if I realistically can afford the time, I refuse. Hours fly by without my remembering to take a break, and often, at night, when the children are home, I'm mentally still at work."

As you lose perspective, you also lose patience and your sense of humor. And you miss the beauty of life's subtler hues.

NONTRANSFERABLE CREDITS

"As vice president of my division I head a staff of fifty, but if my kitchen floor is sticky, I end up feeling like a failure."

Regardless of how high women climb, it takes about one minute to fall off the mountain. Most men in this society look to career as their primary source of self-esteem. A woman, on the other hand, bases her identity on multiple roles: friend, worker, wife, mother, homemaker, teacher, nurturer, lover, community giver, to name a few.

It might seem that having so many irons in the fire increases the potential for positive self-esteem. But not for someone determined to prove herself indispensable. Taking on more roles can simply raise the stakes for failing to live up to high expectations. We set up rigid standards of what constitutes an acceptable performance in every area we deem important. When we have the opportunity to take pleasure in our accomplishments, instead of doing so we focus on those parts of our lives that need improvement. In the eyes of the Indispensable Woman, the cup almost always appears half-empty.

Anna, after twenty years in her field, has won kudos for innovative research and teaching techniques, but her failure to remarry leaves her lonely and depressed. Suzanne is so furious at herself for missing exercise class two weeks in a row, she brushes aside and doesn't hear her friends' compliments for finally losing the fifteen pounds she's been carrying since adolescence. Betsy feels confident and in charge during the two hours spent with her children at home before dropping them at the day-care center. Yet after a half hour of struggling with the new word-processing equipment at work, she's sure she'll never amount to anything. Emma, an award-winning photographer, spends so much time fussing with the fit of her new Japanese kimono that she misses the first half-hour of her opening.

These and other accomplished women appear to have plenty in their lives from which to derive happiness and fulfillment. But instead of savoring their "high marks," they are haunted by their "incompletes." Success in one area *doesn't transfer* to another. In fact, doing well reinforces the cycle of perfectionism.

SELF-EFFACEMENT/ GRANDIOSITY

The Indispensable Woman swings back and forth between diminishing her own worth and presenting an inflated image of importance.

While others may be openly admiring of you, your expectations make it impossible to appreciate yourself. Feelings of inadequacy translate into pressure. No matter how much you give, it doesn't feel like enough; the insecurity fuels an exhausting spiral of diminishing returns.

Eight years ago, after graduating from a small midwestern college, Audrey and her husband moved to Minneapolis, where he went to work at a law firm. A year and a half into their marriage, they decided they wanted a baby. Audrey worked at her job as a dental technician right up until she delivered. After her second child was born, she devoted herself full-time to motherhood.

My first encounter with Audrey was when she called to ask if I could drive a carpool of kids on the nursery school field trip. Audrey belonged to the education committee and was in charge of parent volunteers. In between caring for her three-year-old son and five-year-old daughter, she chaired the synagogue's new members committee, collected door-to-door for the American Cancer Drive, and was famous for the date bars she provided Friday nights after services.

I ran into Audrey one morning in the school parking lot. "How about soliciting for the new building fund?" she asked breathlessly, her arms overflowing with papers. I told her I was up against a deadline, so now just wasn't a good time. "I don't know how you manage to work," she sighed. "It's all I can do to take care of my children."

"But look at everything *you* do," I reminded her. "I'm impressed by how many things you're involved in." Audrey shook her head in disbelief. She explained that the reason she did so much volunteer work was that she didn't feel particularly qualified to do anything else. Being asked to sit on committees made her feel important and respected, confided Audrey. "Besides, someone has to do it," she said laughingly. "I wouldn't dream of saying no."

Audrey made herself indispensable by saying yes whenever asked, and then underrating her contribution.

I encouraged Audrey to take a closer look at all her accomplishments and priorities. Other women achieve the same end through an opposite route—by embellishing their own importance.

Lisa took pride in her ability to handle twelve different things at once. In her usual wry manner, she shared her nickname with the other members of our focus group: Ms. Fix-it. After hearing her extensive list of responsibilities, the others were suitably impressed.

But later, when discussing whether she could get away for the weekend for her tenth-year college reunion, her normally smooth demeanor showed a crack.

"How can I go anywhere?" she asked bitterly. "If, God forbid, I'm sick and need to take a few hours off, everything falls apart. If I miss time at work, my records get screwed up and I have to spend twice the time fixing them when I get back. And forget about the mess at home. Without me, the kids would eat Froot Loops for dinner and the hamper would burst before anyone thought to empty it."

"Maybe you could do more work ahead of time," suggested one participant. "Or what if you hired someone to come in for a few days?" asked another. "Wait a minute," I said. "So what if the kids eat Froot Loops for two days and the laundry sits?" Lisa began to cry quietly. "They can't live without me and if they can, then what do they need me for?"

Lisa had created a monster. She had made herself so central that it seemed impossible to extricate herself even for a short time. Furthermore, the very idea that her absence *wouldn't* automatically signal a disaster made her terrified to leave.

Self-effacement and grandiosity are two sides of the same coin. For some women, putting themselves down is the familiar, well-worn mode. Acting grandiose, as if things cannot run without you, is a less obvious but equally common expression of perfectionism. Both misperceptions can be corrected and are part of recovery.

THE NEED TO
PROVE YOURSELF
▼

When you lack confidence, you are unable to set reasonable limits without worrying that doing so reflects poorly on yourself. To the Indispensable Woman, the word "no" implies incompetence and symbolizes defeat. You stack responsibility upon responsibility, staggering beneath the weight before admitting anything is beyond reach. You *over*do, so that no one can possibly question your ability or worth. Secretly, you hope they'll wonder how they ever got along without you.

Women of past generations, whose roles were more narrowly delineated, certainly felt compelled to prove their worth. But women today, in the process of assuming multilayered roles, feel an overwhelming need to prove they are able to handle the competing demands of relationships, a career, and home life. They continually feel on the line to demonstrate love for family, commitment to a career, and, at all times, finesse at shifting gears swiftly and gracefully.

It's natural for women to feel specially driven to prove themselves at work, one area where they have consistently had to try harder and achieve more than men in order to gain equitable power and remuneration. However, many women feel just as pressing a need to justify choosing a more traditional role. One new mother, at the one-year reunion of her Expecting Change group, announced she was no longer managing her uncle's wholesale record company. But instead of saying she was now staying home raising her child, she announced her new position as director and head teacher at a very private, on-site day-care center with an enrollment of one: her son. After so many years of basing her identity on her career, just being a mother didn't feel important enough.

Another woman in the same group, Polly, shared similar feelings, although her situation was the exact opposite. Polly felt well-prepared going into negotiating her maternity leave. The other receptionists in the office had all taken at least two months off when their babies were born, so she felt fairly confident of being able to do the same. But while meeting with her supervisor, he said something that bothered her, although she tried to forget it. "Don't be gone too long," he jokingly admonished. "Of course, once you see that baby, you probably won't want to come back at all."

During her leave, Polly worried about what she was missing, and whether she was missed. She abbreviated her leave to five weeks, and though she was surprised by how hard it was to leave her son, Adam, she returned to work doubly determined to do a good job. She said, "I wanted to show my boss that being a mom doesn't have to get in the way of my work!"

But Polly was torn. She tried to make up for her guilt at leaving Adam with the babysitter by bringing him special gifts and letting him stay up way past his bedtime. At work, whenever possible, Polly volunteered for extra assignments, so as to squelch any notion that having a baby meant she was less devoted. She was careful not to let her exhaustion show, even when she'd been up several times during the night while Adam was cutting teeth. She just put on more makeup.

While Polly's need to prove herself at work originated with her reaction to her supervisor's insensitive comments, eventually, she was driven by a need to prove her worth to *herself*. Similarly, while Adam may have responded positively to her added gestures of attention, Polly's determination to show she was a good mother came from her own feeling of inadequacy, not from any need he was communicating. And no matter how much she did, at work or at home, she still wasn't able to dispel her anxiety by convincing herself she was a good enough employee *and* mother.

Accomplishments are our trophies, the evidence that we can do whatever we set out to. But the relief they provide is temporary, lasting only until the next challenge presents itself.

It's painful always to feel as if we need to show ourselves and the world that we are good enough, smart enough, loving enough. Having to prove ourselves is a defensive posture; we hide our doubts, pad our achievements, and jockey for position, trying to earn what is already rightfully ours. The challenge is to believe it.

CO-DEPENDENCE

The misconception that you are responsible for another person's feelings or they for yours, is at the core of what has come to be called co-dependent behavior. The Indispensable Woman has trouble establishing clear, appropriate boundaries and overly identifies with other people's problems.

Women in our culture tend to be especially co-dependent. We learn at a young age to be compliant, cooperative, and to please others.

Co-dependence is hard to pin down because it masquerades as caring. You may honestly believe—and convince others—that you are acting out of the goodness of your heart, while you are actually being manipulative and controlling.

Like Vivian, who told the following story: "Early in our marriage, I made the mistake of thinking it was my job to see that Hank looked nice. It was December and we were getting ready for the annual holiday party at work when I noticed he was wearing corduroys and a sweater. 'This is a dress-up affair, honey,' I informed him. 'Why don't you get your good gray suit and I'll iron it for you.'

"'I'm fine with what I have on,' he replied.

"I took out the suit, muttering that he should have had his clothes ready ahead of time. 'You'll be embarrassed wearing that,' I tried to convince him. '*I'm* perfectly comfortable,' he corrected me. 'Don't you mean *you'll* be embarrassed?'"

Vivian came to realize she wasn't responsible for how Hank dressed.

So often we expend great sums of time, energy, and emotion on other people's account, and expect to be appreciated for it, regardless of whether they wanted all that attention. We encourage others to become dependent, while avoiding focusing on our own issues. Ultimately, we aren't doing anyone a favor.

INABILITY TO ASK FOR OR ACCEPT SUPPORT

We've all known someone who is terribly independent. Like trying to buy a gift for the person who has everything, it's practically impossible to offer help to someone who doesn't seem to need it.

There's no one who can use help or support as much as the Indispensable Woman. And there's no one who finds it more difficult to ask.

Being needy or dependent is at direct odds with how the Indispensable Woman wishes to be perceived. She perpetuates an image of self-sufficiency, rarely asking for help and refusing it when offered. It's not because she's pigheaded; she genuinely doesn't know she needs help. She would rather handle everything herself.

There are times when depending on yourself *is* the simpler or better solution. However, this may also be a smokescreen, hiding feelings of vulnerability. Louise, a sensitive, middle-aged Southerner, described how difficult it is for her to accept support: "At work, if I am confused or don't understand something, when someone offers to help, I usually feel ridiculous and angry at the same time. In more personal encounters, when I let anyone in and that person acts warm or caring, I'm sure I'll break down and start crying. It makes me feel about three years old."

Louise seems to believe that being a mature adult requires always going it alone. Becoming indispensable means making believe you are omnipotent, when in fact, like everyone, you need and deserve as much support as you can get. And then some.

It is unlikely that you see in yourself each and every aspect of the Indispensable Woman. Some are bound to hit closer to home than others. When your response to certain characteristics is: "That's me to a T!" pay extra attention. We each have our old dependable patterns of coping. Yours may be to withdraw and deny yourself support. Another person might become more compulsively overextended.

Since making yourself indispensable happens progressively, it's also important to note how you've changed over time. Are you more or less fragmented than you were six months ago? A year ago? Do you find it increasingly difficult to ask for support? Can you remember a time when people's opinions of you didn't seem to matter so much?

As you read through each characteristic, you may feel overwhelmed, alarmed, or even relieved by the descriptions. If reading them adds to your feelings of pressure, rest assured that identification is the beginning stage of any process of recovery. And give yourself credit for your willingness to look!

THREE

HIDDEN
PRESSURE

By now you might be thinking, "It would be nice to have the luxury to do less, but if I don't take care of things, who will?" Or as one woman said, "It's going to take a heck of a lot to convince me that I'm *not* indispensable."

Attempting to persuade you that you aren't indispensable, that it's possible to relinquish some of your responsibilities, is fruitless, and anyway, it's beside the point. Contrary to popular belief, your responsibilities aren't the direct cause of your pressure. You are.

When we feel anxious, stressed, and overburdened, most of us point a finger at one of two things: having too much responsibility or receiving too many demands from other people. We cite these reasons as if they were nonnegotiable facts of life.

There *are* times in our lives when too much is being asked of us. We've all experienced periods when we just plain reach our limit; the thought of one more thing to cope with threatens to push us over the edge. For women who make themselves indispensable, exorbitant demands are the norm.

The amount of responsibility we Indispensable Women carry matters less than how we respond to it. We look at the legitimate pressures in our lives, then exaggerate them until they become overwhelming. Instead of being relaxed and matter-of-fact about what we have to get done, we get all wound up with performing perfectly, which in turn creates more pressure.

Responsibility *isn't* synonymous with pressure. It *is* true that the more you take on, the more you have to be concerned about, but have you ever noticed that you can have ten different things to do, and still, if you're organized and in the right mood, you enjoy them all and somehow everything goes smoothly? On the other hand, if your mind is filled with chaos or conflict, you can bask in the sun and still feel like a wreck.

Consider the numbers of women who drop out of high-level careers, then transfer their tension into relationships, redecorating their homes, or worrying about whether their children are achieving. It's common to hold tightly to pressure, even when actual tasks have been delegated or put aside. Some people even experience "vacation anxiety syndrome," the irrational fear your position will be eliminated while you're away.

If there's too much responsibility in your life, it's most likely because, in one way or another, you've chosen it. Likewise, you can learn to give some of it up. We assume too much responsibility because of what it gives us. Having a lot of responsibility can be the difference between being isolated and being needed, between feeling inadequate and feeling important.

Helen, an impressive woman in her late forties, owns a tele-marketing company. She is typical of women for whom excessive responsibility is a statement of self-worth. As we talked, I was impressed by Helen's honesty and insight. She was sharp enough to realize her stress level was beginning to interfere with her marriage, but she wasn't able to see how she had actively chosen a lifestyle that compounded her pressure.

Helen is not a Harvard MBA–model career woman. She barely completed two years of college before marrying, and the only job she ever held before having a baby was as a part-time sales clerk. She devoted herself to mothering, housekeeping, and putting together an antique collection she was terribly proud of.

Around the time her oldest child started college, Helen decided she wanted a job. Not a part-time, fill-in-the-hours job, but a real career, with responsibility, status, and more than a token paycheck. She approached a friend of the family and asked for a job selling for his telemarketing company.

For the first time in years, Helen got up before ten A.M. She threw herself into the job with a vengeance, trying to learn all aspects so she would be more knowledgeable. Before long she was earning a substantial salary. Three years after she started, the owner had a stroke. Helen and her husband bought the business and she took over at the helm.

Within twelve months, the company's profits were up almost a hundred percent. So was Helen's work load. Before, her job had meant a great deal. Now it seemed to be the only thing that mattered. It was not unusual for her to rush in late for dinner, her anxiety about a particular account the entire focus of the evening's conversation. If it had been a good day, she was euphoric; if there'd been any hassles, she was impossible to be around. She was so wrapped up in the business she'd become snappish and impatient with her husband and their fourteen-year-old son. They were starting to feel like innocent victims in a combat zone.

Although Helen took on a particularly demanding challenge, her story is not unique. She complains bitterly of being overburdened, saying, "Some days there are so many problems, I wish I could just fire everybody and do their jobs myself." But she is also able to see that the continual crisis management is stimulating; it makes her feel important.

Helen's dilemma illustrates the Indispensable Woman's difficulty in moderating her need to achieve. And her situation is complicated by her need to make up for lost time. The same is true of how we, as Indispensable Women, handle other people's demands. While we complain about how much everyone asks and expects, more often than not, *we've* established their expectations. We allow ourselves to be recruited and drawn in. Or we make ourselves indispensable by soliciting opportunities to help, fix, or solve problems.

Certainly there are those instances in which it's compulsory to respond—when a supervisor assigns work or a child's basic needs are involved. Perfectionists, however, can't discriminate between the mandatory and the optional. We're on the scene at every signal of distress, for fear of being judged inconsiderate or lacking in commitment if we're not. We may welcome others' demands— or swallow our resentment and grudgingly do what is asked. In either case, we're shaking hands on the deal. *We* are responsible for our mounting feelings of pressure.

Women report frequent bouts of anxiety with no apparent cause. Even when we add everything up, it still doesn't account for how pressured we feel. Why is it that no amount of organization, support, or even elimination of tasks completely relieves the disquiet that colors our day-to-day lives?

The missing key is a nearly imperceptible element called HIDDEN PRESSURE. It is the underlying sensation you experience, regardless of what's happening on the outside. It is the lingering apprehension at the end of a productive work day or the irrational guilt you feel if your grown children aren't achieving, even though their lives are in their hands. It is the sick feeling you just can't shake when your house isn't perfectly in order, you've been slow to return a phone call to your mother, or you haven't had sufficient time to study for a test.

Hidden pressure is the voice that tells the Indispensable Woman she's simply not done enough.

FIVE FACTS ABOUT HIDDEN PRESSURE

Like waves insistently pounding the shore, a sense of urgency propels us. No amount of reassurance or careful planning appeases the urge to get it done *now*. We are filled with apprehension unless we stay one step ahead of our own agendas.

There are five main reasons for hidden pressure:

- the gap between actual and assumed responsibility;
- the internalizing of expectations;
- an inability to set priorities;
- taking things personally; and
- a lack of a yardstick for measuring success.

ASSUMING TOO MUCH

By believing *everything* is up to her, the Indispensable Woman assumes more than her share. One major cause of hidden pressure is an inability to separate ACTUAL and ASSUMED responsibilities. Actual responsibilities are those tasks or obligations for which you are directly accountable. Assumed responsibilities include everything you've decided is up to you, whether or not it *actually* is.

The difference between actual and assumed responsibility can seem subtle, because you *are* responsible for much of what you *feel* responsible for, and vice versa. One way to think about it is in terms of what you can and cannot control. For example, let's say you handle collections at a large department store. You know what's expected; your actual responsibilities are delineated and clear. It's one thing to be a dedicated employee; however, when you lose sleep fuming about overdue accounts, you move well beyond your realm.

Or maybe you and your husband have devised a schedule whereby each of you is in charge of making dinner three nights a week. When you pull out recipe cards the night before it's his turn to cook and leave them taped to the mirror in the morning, or stop for take-out eggrolls on your way home just in case there isn't enough—that's taking over!

Confusing excellence with perfectionism is another way the Indispensable Woman assumes too much. As was noted in Chapter One, striving for excellence means wanting to do your absolute best. Perfectionism involves a compulsion to exceed your best efforts—to prove your capability, earn admiration, or do so much so well as to be beyond criticism.

I was introduced to Carol, a middle-aged woman, at a neighborhood coffee party. I was immediately struck by her assertive manner. Carol told me she had been head nurse in emergency surgery at a large hospital for the past five years. This was the first weekend she'd had off in six months. "Why such grueling hours?" I asked. "Don't they realize people need time to regroup?"

"Oh, it isn't hospital policy," explained Carol. "I just like to be around, in case anyone needs me or something goes wrong."

As we visited, a picture emerged of a very lonely woman who had invested far too much of herself in her work. Carol's social life revolved around the hospital. Even on her infrequent days off, she worried about how things were going and sometimes detoured from errands to drop in. Her staff admired her dedication, but wished she would lighten up and trust them more.

When I questioned Carol, she informed me in no uncertain terms that her constant presence was essential to the success of the department. "I'm just trying to see that we have the best emergency room in town!" she stressed. "That takes a lot, but it's got to be done."

Carol blamed her pressure on having too much responsibility, but actually her need for connection motivated her to double and triple her duties. At home, she wandered around her apartment feeling lonely and lost. At work, she felt as if she belonged.

I suggested to Carol there was nothing inherently wrong with wanting to excel. But when you can't leave work for fear of putting it in someone else's hands, or when it consumes so much psychic space there's little room for anything else in your life, then your feelings of responsibility are way out of proportion.

It's natural for everything you care about to be misconstrued as part of your actual responsibility. But that's a fallacy. Some things demand your direct input or attention; others can be delegated or aren't your problem to begin with. This exercise will help reveal the gap between what you *are* and what you *feel* responsible for:

1. In your mind or on a sheet of paper, identify several significant roles you play in your life.

2. Next to each role, list every single thing you are actually responsible for. Be as detailed and specific as possible.

3. Now, make a second list of everything you *feel* responsible for. Remember: The first list includes only those things that are actually up to you. The second takes into account anything and everything you worry about or concern yourself with.

While there may be some overlap, your second list is bound to be more extensive. Some of the same items may appear on both lists, but with different levels of intensity. For example, my first list might include responsibility for making my daughter's school lunch. But, according to my second list, it's up to me whether she finishes and *likes* it.

As you analyze your lists, try to isolate those areas where there is the greatest discrepancy between actual and assumed responsibility. You experience greater pressure wherever there is a noticeable gap. For some women it's at work, for others it's in personal relationships. Still other women say they feel inordinately responsible in literally *every* part of their lives.

INTERNALIZED EXPECTATIONS

▼

Your expectations cause the gap between your actual responsibility and what you *feel* responsible for. You may or may not have more responsibility than you want or can handle. Even if your life is perfectly tailored to meet your needs, sky-high expectations create intense feelings of pressure.

Expectations are particularly critical in determining how much responsibility we assume in relationships. Because of our tendency as women to think of ourselves in terms of our various roles—worker, mother, lover, or friend—every task or encounter is approached with some prior expectation that is based on the images and ideas those roles conjure up. For example, in your mind, maybe the perfect wife remembers every special occasion on both sides of the family, or a good friend always has time to listen. Perhaps you believe a dependable employee never makes a mistake and a self-respecting woman always looks presentable— meaning, well-dressed and perfectly made up.

Indispensable Women have exceptionally high standards. We aren't satisfied with mediocre work or lukewarm relationships. We expect ourselves to stand out, to shine. When our performance isn't up to advance billing, we are disappointed. We may feel angry, sad, afraid, or even ashamed. But instead of acknowledging these feelings, we say we feel pressured, using the phrase as a catchall.

What we call "pressure" is actually the end product of a predictable pattern. When we assume a role, any role, we assign certain responsibilities to it. For example, you might define your parental role to include nurturing, educating, and providing a safe environment for your children. Your definition of a friend may include keeping in touch, being supportive, and celebrating milestones.

Making a commitment to fulfill your responsibilities is one

thing. Gearing up to be "perfect mother" or "best friend" is another. That's where expectations come in.

Because we expect so much, we are extremely self-critical, imposing harsh judgment if we disappoint a friend or lose our temper when a child points his finger down his throat by way of commenting on the dinner we've labored over.

We are terribly hard on ourselves. One woman says it took nearly a month to forgive herself for forgetting to send a card to her aunt in the hospital. The first time I had a serious fight with my high-school boyfriend, I was so grief-stricken, I insisted my mother drive me to his house in the middle of the night so I could apologize.

Instead of rating on a continuum, we grade ourselves pass/fail on every action. When we let ourselves down or judge our performance as imperfect, we feel renewed pressure and embark on new programs. Friends suddenly get extra calls just to catch up; the kids are treated to an increase in "quality time"; we're glad to volunteer our house for the family's Thanksgiving get-together. We redouble our efforts to assure we make the grade.

EVERYTHING BUT
THE KITCHEN SINK

Another reason you feel so pressured is that you can't order the importance of all the different things vying for your attention. Everything, whether it's feeding the cat or getting the account you've been working on, feels equally pressing. It's hard to pinpoint the exact source of your tension.

Marge, an editor at a magazine in New York, describes herself as being "really into my career." The hectic pace of the publishing world is compatible with her high-strung personality, and though she complains about the pressure, she secretly thrives on it.

Because her job is so demanding, Marge uses her weekends

to get everything else done. By Saturday morning, a long list of domestic chores has accumulated—grocery shopping, doing the laundry, and working in the garden, not to mention making home improvements. Right after breakfast Marge flies around the house like a whirling dervish, collecting used coffee cups and trying to keep her balance carting loads of laundry down the stairs. In the meantime, her six-year-old daughter begs for attention, which she tries disjointedly to give.

"All that can wait," implored her husband Jack one Sunday afternoon, trying to convince Marge to quit straightening up and accompany them on a walk.

"It would get done a lot faster if you'd help," snapped Marge.

"But I couldn't care less about whether the cupboards have new shelf-paper," he said. "Why should I spend my precious time worrying about it when I could be enjoying the day with you?"

Marge mistakenly believes most of her pressure stems from her large work load at the office, when it's really more tied up with what happens at home. At her job, she sets reachable goals and enjoys her success. But because she's insecure in her role as a homemaker, she isn't able to figure out what can and can't wait. Having been raised by a mother whose kitchen floors were clean enough to eat off, Marge feels like a failure by comparison. She blocks out everything around her but the task at hand, including her husband's gestures of warmth. She's unable to enjoy herself until everything's finished, and then, only as long as it remains neat.

Since there's no way to do it all, if you can't set priorities, you're bound to feel overpowered. Prioritizing implies compromise: an acceptance of limitations and a willingness to live with them. In *Women and Self-Esteem: Understanding and Improving the Way We Think and Feel About Ourselves,* authors Sanford and Donovan state: "Women with expectations of perfection often feel compelled to be 'the best' in virtually *all* areas as opposed to having realistic goals in a few carefully chosen areas. As a result, self-satisfaction is generally impossible. Because nothing in the world is ever perfect, her jobs are never done."[1]

The Indispensable Woman is loath to admit there's anything she can't do. Keeping her hand in helps maintain an illusion of control, even if on the inside she's coming apart—or suffering in silence. Because everything is equally urgent, if she completes one task, she feels just as pressured to tackle the rest. Each concern is of top-level importance, so putting anything aside or forgetting about it for a while is out of the question.

TAKING IT PERSONALLY . . .

▼

Women are famous for taking everything to heart. The sideways glance or Freudian slip becomes one more thing to worry about. Feedback is often misinterpreted as criticism, and when something is wrong, we automatically assume it's our fault.

If you take something personally, you have a heartfelt interest and investment in its outcome. But the Indispensable Woman becomes involved in and feels responsible for more than her share. She thinks she is the cause and the cure, when more often than not, she is merely a bystander.

Taking things personally is really a way of trying to be in control. When a loved one is hurting or in need, it is wrenching to feel helpless in the face of that person's pain. We want to do something, anything to actively bring an end to his suffering.

Even if you aren't compelled to action, taking things personally increases the pressure you feel. I recently overheard a woman in a restaurant discussing her day. She went on in great detail: "Everything started out fine. I got up in plenty of time for breakfast, and the sun was shining when I started off to work. I was mentally rehearsing my sales presentation when suddenly the traffic slowed to a halt. There had been an accident and I was going to be late. The guy in the next lane honked and glared as if I'd inched him out of the marathon. If I'd left fifteen minutes earlier, this wouldn't have happened.

"The sales meeting had already started when I got there. You should have seen Bob's face. If looks could kill! I could tell he was furious, and then I gave my presentation and no one said anything, so it must have been a flop. Then I met my sister for lunch to help her write her résumé and she said Mom's been depressed ever since she heard I'm breaking things off with Herb. I knew I shouldn't have told her."

This woman sees everything in relation to herself. She needs to stop taking things personally that are beyond her control.

OFF THE SCALE

In some ways the Indispensable Woman is a contradiction in terms; on the one hand, she appears to be in charge, yet she gives away her power by allowing others to determine her worth.

Women, in general, don't put enough stock in our individual judgment. Because we have been taught to look outside ourselves for validation, when it comes to measuring our success, we lack critical tools. We are vulnerable to real, implied, or imagined criticism and fickle when it comes to trusting our own perception of reality. We're quick to accept other people's opinions as carrying more weight than our own.

Without reliable internal yardsticks it is impossible to know when to ask for assistance and when to consider ourselves the authority, when to try harder and when to pat ourselves on the back. We unwittingly contribute to hidden pressure because of an inability to know when we've achieved our goals, and when to accept, acknowledge, and applaud our accomplishments.

Giving away your power by putting your self-worth in other people's hands places you in a precarious position. No one is entirely objective, and besides, it isn't up to someone else to decide if you're okay.

Creating usable measures is a must if the Indispensable Woman is to stop worrying and endlessly trying to prove herself. Later chapters will offer steps toward devising realistic and appropriate standards.

We can't change or control other people's expectations, but we can work to present a more honest picture of who we are. To do so, we need to understand how our expectations are formed. Where did we get the idea that we have to be perfect? How did we come to expect so much of ourselves?

FOUR

THE ROOTS OF PERFECTIONISM

Every once in a while I make a deal with myself, an informal contract to slow down and give myself some rope. I vow to make only commitments I can keep and stop upsetting myself over what isn't finished. Then I cheat, pushing up deadlines or furtively squeezing in one more potential accomplishment. I hurriedly wash dishes while pretending to listen raptly as a friend chatters away on the other end of the line. Days off, meant for relaxing, instead are taken up with long-neglected projects. Trying to do nothing is so nerve-racking, it's a relief to go back to work! Even the peace of nighttime is interrupted by mental list-making and worrying. I try to stop pushing myself, but to no avail.

At various points in your life, you too may have made an effort to prioritize, scale back expectations, and quit making yourself indispensable. Rationally, you know you don't have to be perfect. Despite this, an inner voice urges you on: "If you just try harder, give a little more, *anything* is possible."

Consciously, we acknowledge our limitations, but the real struggle is with deep-seated needs that motivate and move us. As far back as I can remember, I have wanted to be more. Regardless of how I'm doing or what anyone says, I yearn to be better, prettier, smarter, so I may find the love and acceptance I so desperately crave.

Conditioning is at the root of female perfectionism. We are all, from the instant of birth, exposed to countless messages that shape our beliefs, attitudes, and values. As newborns, our self-esteem is first formed by how we are fed, changed, and held. Later, at the onset of formal education, we are socialized and specifically taught how to think and what is worth thinking about. Religious upbringing further instills a value system, providing larger-than-life role models—and miracles for emphasis. Above all else, our earliest, most intense and pervasive messages come from our families, where we learn how to be and how to love and how to be loved.

It is the rare, perhaps nonexistent individual who can boast of having experienced unqualified love as a child. The unspoken yet well-understood conditions for love and acceptance are internalized and carried into adulthood. (In Freudian terms, this is the "super-ego," or conscience that arbitrates appropriate and acceptable behavior.) The external rules of childhood become the inner voices informing our conduct in the world beyond the family—how to dress, to eat, to act, even how to feel. "If I only figure out the right way to be, they will love me" and "If I can just be good enough, he won't leave me" are the emotional phrases underlying our behavior. From birth to death, we are engaged in an effort to meet the conditions that will ensure security and guard against abandonment.

Because we have been taught that love is earned, naturally we set out to win our portion by trying to measure up to the conditions or standards initially set by our parents, and then re-created internally. Instead of acting out of deeply held knowledge of our own validity as individuals, our psyches, and in turn, our behavior, become twisted and misshapen into some semblance of what we believe we *must* be. The absolute authenticity of self that we are born with gradually disappears behind an outer shell designed for approval and acceptance.

The theme of conditional self-worth is present in the three most primary influences in life: THE FAMILY; SOCIAL SHAP-

ING; and RELIGIOUS UPBRINGING. We will examine the messages we received from each of these to understand the part they play in forming our expectations.

THE FAMILY

A discussion of the significance of the family system in the history of psychiatry is hardly needed to convince anyone that our parents have a huge impact on us. Suffice it to say that the family is the primary force in shaping the deepest layer of who we are and how we feel about ourselves. Anyone who has been in therapy has spent time on the subject. Those who have never been involved in a formal process of self-analysis have certainly thought about what it means to have been raised within our own families.

The influence of our families begins at birth, possibly even pre-birth, according to the work of Arthur Janov.[1] In the primal hallway between the womb and the world, we receive a powerful imprint of our vulnerability and dependency. Survival rests on being nourished and protected, which, at life's earliest stage, is totally in the hands of the parents.

Accommodation is the coping mechanism human beings use in order to feel safe and secure in the environment. We continually modify our behavior in the hopes of increasing the chances of getting our needs met. Tiny newborns learn within days, even hours, the best way to rest their mouths around the nipple to assure maximum nourishment. In the same way, small children become wise to winning approval and getting along in the family. Growing up, we quickly learn what conditions must be met to satisfy our parents.

Most parents set out to teach their children social survival skills, bringing the very best of intentions to the task of training their offspring as competent members of society. Because parents are simply older, more experienced human beings, they come bearing their history, usually involving a complex web of unresolved issues and unhealed pain. Consequently, most parents' ambitions for their children are unconsciously tainted with their own, not-so-pure needs.

These needs translate into expectations between parent and child, expectations often intensely loaded with messages about how the child must act in order to be acceptable, lovable. For daughters, the messages usually focus on three central themes: "niceness," dependence/independence, and physical appearance.

Being a "good" girl or a "nice" girl or any version of the same is one of the most universal messages given female children. Traditional interpretations of femininity rely heavily on the concept of niceness. If given the sentence, "Nice girls . . ." to complete, few women would come up with a blank.

While their brothers are also admonished to be "nice boys," the definition differs quite a bit between genders. For females, nice usually means polite, passive, and acquiescent. Girls are encouraged to be highly aware of their manners and to cultivate a deferential air that will be pleasing to others. While boys may be told to "mind their manners," a certain amount of rough-and-tumble boisterousness and mischief are looked on with approval.

Niceness is also defined as giving to others. The female conditioning to be caring and empathetic originates in the family. In her research, Nancy Chodorow traces the emphasis on giving to early childhood, when the female child experiences herself as like her mother, and thus identifies; whereas for the male child, the challenge is to separate from his mother. As a result, she says, "Girls emerge from this period with a basis for 'empathy' built in to their primary definition of self in a way boys do not."[2] Dr. Jean Baker Miller, in *Toward a New Psychology of Women,* says, "Women have different organizing principles around which their psyches are structured. One of these principles is that they exist to serve other people's needs."[3]

While many families today are actively working on overcoming sex-role stereotyping, most of us were raised in an era when it was perfectly acceptable (and expected) to treat boys and girls differently. The clear message that being a good and nice person entailed being empathetic, care-taking, and other-oriented was impressed upon every woman I interviewed. Overwhelmingly, women associated feelings of pressure with the expectation to prove their niceness with acts of giving and goodness. Guilt resulted when they weren't, for one reason or another, able to give enough.

Being nice also implies the absence of any troubles, problems, blemishes, and "bad" feelings. All of us who have struggled with facing the flaws in our families, with expressing anger, with looking into the darkest crevasses of our personalities, know that "good girls" aren't supposed to think about, much less delve into, these areas. The conditioning to suppress the part of ourselves that is complicated and messy and troublesome, namely our sexuality, sounded loud and clear, especially during adolescence. Here, the message was, sexuality is something to be either ashamed of, terrified of, or ignored, coupled with, above all else, don't get into trouble. Nice girls simply didn't. But at the same time, nice girls were trained to use their sexuality to attract males, by being seductive and coquettish. Again, the confusing double bind: we were taught only to relate to our bodies within rigid and prescribed expectations, separate from our own pleasure. Many of us couldn't figure out whether to be good or bad and which was which.

The differences between male and female conditioning were accentuated between adolescence and adulthood in dealing with issues of dependence and independence. This is one area where messages given females are racked with contradictions. Girls are typically overprotected and their dependency is encouraged. Traditionally parents have been far quicker to restrict their daughters' access and freedom, for fear of their being hurt.

In *The Cinderella Complex,* Colette Dowling looked at reasons for women's hidden fear of independence. She explains, "Adults do not interfere with or thwart the instinctual behavior of girls—*except for their gropings toward independence.* These they systematically stymie—as if their girl children, by reaching out and taking chances, were courting death itself."[4] However, Nancy

Friday, in *My Mother/Myself,* reveals another dynamic that might account for the apparently mixed messages female children and adolescents receive, particularly from their mothers. According to Friday, mothers are torn between feeling it is their responsibility to prepare their daughters for the inevitable hardships of being female in order to protect them, and wanting their daughters to transcend the limitations they experienced—to go beyond the mother in growth, exploration, and experience.[5]

So on the one hand, we are given a clear message that we must be careful, not venture too far, be docile and dependent if we are to be acceptable, lovable daughters. But still, we are expected to achieve, perhaps even to outdistance our own mothers. As adults, this pull and push between dependence and independence forms the basis of much inner conflict. Not knowing whether to hold back or come forth, whether to concentrate on taking care of others or to fulfill our own needs, we are constantly in turmoil, unable to feel completely content with how we are choosing to live and where we are putting our energy.

The conditioning to be nice and to walk a tightrope between dependence and independence created heavy pressures for most women. Added to these was the emphasis on physical appearance that most women recall as fundamental in their upbringing. Being pretty was a goal many parents set, supported, and, in some cases, pursued with a vengeance, spending thousands of dollars on haircuts, fashionable wardrobes, and, in the most extreme cases, even plastic surgery. At my suburban junior high school, eight of my classmates returned from Christmas vacation one year with newly sculptured noses.

The pressure to look good starts early, when little girls are fussed over and primped, so that the parents will enjoy the ensuing compliments. "What a pretty little girl!" Unfortunately, when good looks, which are always defined in terms of what is culturally fashionable, are equated with an individual's worth, the result is serious self-esteem problems, including difficulties in coping, dysfunctional relationships, and eating habits ranging from compulsive dieting to life-threatening disorders. Problems that originate in childhood may not surface until later years.

* * *

Naomi's voice shook when she called to make her first appointment with a psychotherapist. Five days later, seated in the therapist's office, Naomi tentatively began to share her story.

She had come because of depression. After what seemed like a promising start, her latest relationship had ended like all the others before it. Naomi couldn't understand why her efforts at romance failed. She talked about her first marriage, which had disintegrated after three very bumpy years, and the series of men she had met and slept with, who all seemed to like her at first, then gradually tire of her. When Timothy, her most recent boyfriend, complimented her or told her he loved her, she would say something sarcastic or flare up in a rage, convinced he must be either stupid or lying. His parting words were the suggestion she should "find someone who would hate her as much as she hated herself."

Naomi's difficulty maintaining a relationship was one symptom of low self-esteem. The oldest daughter of wealthy parents of European descent, Naomi was brought up in an affluent suburb of Philadelphia. Her father's position with a large corporation secured more than enough income to provide a luxurious life-style. Her third birthday party featured a sit-down luncheon complete with a clown and a life-size playhouse. As a teenager, she and her mother regularly went to New York for shopping sprees.

A statuesque, brittle woman, Naomi's mother had dropped out of college in the middle of her junior year to marry. She conceived within two months of the honeymoon and abandoned her dream of being a painter, instead devoting her energy to volunteer work and philanthropy. Her attraction to beautiful objects was transferred to her small daughter, whom she proudly referred to as "my dear little doll." She dressed Naomi in dainty white pinafores, never allowing her to play in the sandbox or, as she got older, to leave the house without a ribbon in her hair. She was a stickler for good manners, which she called "breeding," and pushed Naomi to study so she would be at the top of her class.

Three weeks into the sessions, Naomi seemed eager to talk about her family. Her hazel eyes softened as she described an idyllic childhood: "a paradise of wonderful toys and fancy dresses."

But they clouded over as she recalled an incident that occurred when she was nine. "It was recess and most of the kids were out on the playground playing running tag. One of the boys, I think his name was Randy, was 'it.' He was after me and when he caught up, he tagged me so hard I tripped and fell right into some mud, which got all over my dress, my face, and into my hair. I was such a mess the teacher sent me home. When I opened the door, all these ladies were sitting around the dining room table. My mother was hosting a luncheon. As soon as she saw me, she rushed over, but she didn't hold me or help me get out of my dirty clothes, even though I was shivering. I tried to tell her what had happened, but she just looked embarrassed and gave me a little shove up the stairs. Then I overheard her say, 'I can't imagine what happened. Naomi usually looks so nice!' "

As she told her story, Naomi's shoulders relaxed and her eyes filled with tears. The relief of allowing herself to feel opened the way for other early memories of hurt. She had never felt truly accepted by her mother. When Naomi did something well, her mother lavished affection, but her intolerance for even the slightest infraction was expressed by biting criticism or stony withdrawal.

Naomi's early self-confidence was contingent on her mother's approval, and later, on the feedback of her close friends. Like many young women desperate for acceptance, she became overly dependent on her relationships. But the real rub, and the main issue she grappled with in therapy, was her inability to accept love and support when offered. She ultimately pushed away those who loved her, sabotaging the very thing she needed and craved. Once Naomi was able to see how she had internalized her mother's intolerance, she began working to free herself of its continuing hold.

Naomi's story isn't out of the ordinary. We all have our versions of the ways in which our parents failed, to whatever degree, to grant us full acceptance.

How rare the parent who spontaneously embraces his or her kindergartner, saying, "I love you, just because you're you!" Instead, children are cautioned to sit quietly, brush their hair, or study so that they will be popular or do well in school. Continually admonished to do things for their own good, children sense their parents' underlying hopes and dreams.

I have often used the term "payback kids" to talk about parents' investment in their children's success as a way of making up for their own losses or failures. Our parents wanted to provide the material security they didn't have. Today, I catch myself and other members of my generation doing the same thing, only instead, we are adamantly invested in our children's emotional security. More than once I have had to back off after trying to corner my six-year-old into an honest, meaningful heart-to-heart, when she'd rather watch *Sesame Street*.

Being a parent, I am struck again and again by the challenge of rearing children: wanting them to have all that the world offers, while loving them enough to accept them as they are. Just moments after Zoe's birth, as I held her in my arms, I had one and only one thought: Here is a perfect human being.

Since that first breathtaking moment, I have realized that like everyone else, my daughter is human. And as I become intimate with my children's flaws and imperfections, I rediscover my own.

Before a child's inexperienced eyes, parents appear omnipotent. I carry a hazy, pleasant mental picture of my mother across the room, absorbed in her work. Her figure seems regal and imposing; I am bathed in her utter authority, which I count on with the same certainty that the sun will rise and I with it.

Perhaps the most ironic twist in the relationship between parent and child is how reticent parents are in admitting their faults. They go to great lengths to conceal doubts and fears, pretending to be all-knowing, thinking they are protecting their children. But they do a great disservice. It is a comfort to realize that the people we most respect and depend on have rough spots and irregular corners.

Learning to live with imperfection is a worthwhile lesson. What greater gift for a child than to have her parents openly acknowledge their humanness? What better way to learn that the real business of life is to keep trying, not to pretend we are already there.

Only by giving up our childlike expectations of our parents' perfection, can we forgive them and move on. And by forgiving our parents, we come closer to forgiving ourselves for not being perfect either.

Coming to terms with the messages we received in our families is a long-term process, requiring commitment to honest examination, sometimes with the help of a skilled therapist. Even when therapy isn't precipitated by a crisis or a chronic problem, unraveling your parents' role in your emotional makeup is instructive and revealing.

SOCIAL SHAPING

From the moment a pink ribbon is lovingly tied around the crib bars, expected norms for female behavior begin to be laid down. While the family is by far the primary influence, social forces have a big impact on who we are and what we strive to become. As we grow, we absorb the popular images, roles, and rules for being girls, and later, women. By the time we are three years old, although we may fantasy-play at being the opposite sex, most children are clearly gender identified[6] and have developed some fairly distinctive ideas of the differences between the sexes.

Acceptable female behavior is indoctrinated through the family, formal education, the media, and all the other cultural messages that convey the parameters within which women are allowed to move in our society. While the status of women slowly improves, we were all raised in an era when women's voices carried little weight. Historically, women have systematically been denied access to power and control outside the realm of domesticity. Individual circumstances aside, all women, to one degree or another, have been taught to see themselves as "second-class citizens."

In response, women feel pressured to prove—through indispensability and overperformance—that nothing is beyond our scope, that we can meet and succeed at any and all challenges.

Remaining doubts that women can hold our own are brushed aside. Similar to the famous Avis Rent A Car slogan, being in second place, we have to try harder.

LEARNING
THE ROPES

Over the past century, in most families, mother's primary role was homemaker and care-giver. The socialization process continued in school, where for most of us Dick and Jane represented the order of the day. Along with sex role stereotyping and history books that almost exclusively lauded the accomplishments of men (thank goodness for Betsy Ross and her needle or we'd have been left out of the Revolution altogether) young girls were given two equally forceful yet contradictory messages: good girls don't make waves, and, in order to be taken seriously, it is necessary to try harder and to do more.

By the tender age of eight, I was acutely aware of this conflict. At the onset of each school year, I vowed to bite my tongue and forcibly restrain my arm from shooting up whenever the teacher posed a question. Because quiet, shy girls seemed to have that special something (little did I know I was up against age-old conditioning), I tried to rein in my enthusiasm and natural self-assurance, even toying with the idea of changing my name to Lynn, which somehow seemed more ladylike and docile. Still, I did raise my hand, and often, even though it felt risky to do so. It has been well-documented that boys are encouraged to leap right in and, in general, receive greater amounts of attention from teachers in the classroom.[7]

Little girls who were my classmates have grown up to become everything from single heads of households to heads of corporations, still struggling to make sense of the conflicting urges to sit still or take a stand, to speak out or shut up, knowing that either choice costs them dearly.

And we are torn in other ways. We continually feel forced to choose between work and family or love relationships; financial and worldly aspirations battle the longing to nourish and sustain our softer, more spiritual side. We struggle with clashing needs to settle down and establish order and stability without losing the capacity for romance, spontaneity, and full expression of our sexuality. We criticize and rip at the constraints of past eras, but contemporary society still falls short of supporting women in finding creative ways to balance and fulfill all sides of ourselves.

THE POLITICS
OF PRESSURE

Regardless of our success in the world of work, social conditioning says that in order to be a good woman, a successful woman, a *real* woman, it is necessary to embody the roles of nurturer and care-giver, which are doubly reinforced by social/biological imperatives. The potential to give birth and provide for offspring is a powerful pull. Women who choose a different route, because they prefer to remain childfree out of life-style preferences or financial considerations, are often criticized and made to feel inadequate. There is tremendous pressure to conform, as evidenced by the cost to women who choose to go against the grain of marriage, childbearing, or heterosexuality.

Any woman who works to support herself, make a marriage or relationship work, succeed in a career, or be the kind of mother she wants to be, knows that trying to live up to a role is, at best, a temporary road map complete with detours and out-of-the-way turns. At worst, it traps us into trying to be someone other than who we are.

Women in their thirties and forties fault themselves for failing to emulate their own mothers, while struggling to surpass them. Women in mid-life, watching their children leave, wonder whether all the work was worth it. Older women, engrossed in their own aging, are bemused and bewildered by younger women's lives and what they might have missed.

Even when we satisfy some version of what is expected, we continue to be divided against ourselves. Women who can afford and decide to stay with their children are made to feel defensive about living out the very role they were brought up to fulfill. Working mothers who claim to be "liberated" feel guilty about their style of parenting, and unconsciously measure themselves against an outdated model of their own mothers.

Women today, trying to integrate time-honored role models with present ideals, struggle to come to terms. How do we reconcile memories of the fragrance of home-baked bread and family vacations with the reality of frozen dinners and singles dating services? How to run a meeting when your stomach's in knots because your child's at home with the flu?

The fact is, women who were brought up believing that living out their prescribed roles would assure happiness and security are finding this is not the case. The idea that girls automatically grow up to be wives and mothers, and that marriage means being comfortably provided for, is neither based in fact, nor is it something all women aspire to.

ECONOMIC REALITIES

▼

For many women, particularly those with small children, economic dependence is a strong factor in the need to be needed, in the need to be secure. With staggering divorce rates and alimony practically obsolete, many married women are in the precarious position of being but "one man away from poverty."[8]

Women have been making themselves indispensable in relationships for reasons of economic security since the beginning of time. As far back as prehistoric days, women have traded domestic and sexual services for food and shelter in order to ensure their own and their offspring's survival. The modern word for this is "trade-off."

The great majority of our mothers, due to economic dependence, made significant compromises: they became indispensable at home in order to justify being supported by their husbands. By excelling in the domestic domain—childrearing, cooking, cleaning, entertaining—they felt they earned their keep. Women who were financially well-off, who could afford household help, looked elsewhere for areas in which to excel: volunteer work, hobbies, PTA, church, and more lavish entertaining. Beyond justifying financial support, they often felt they had to justify their existence!

Despite remarkable gains due to the women's movement, and even with the inner security of being independent wage-earners, we still buy into many of the expectations handed down by our mothers and perpetuated by stereotyping. Even when we reject outright the traditional subservient female role, we've incorporated the standards and internalized the clichés. However much we scoff at the image of Marabel Morgan's Total Woman" and all she represents, we're still subject to inner voices telling us it's important to create a lovely home despite a long, exhausting day at work and to greet our mate looking fresh and pretty, eager to hear about his day without burdening him with our own problems.

According to authors Martha T. Schuch Mednick and Hilda J. Weissman, "Conceptions of women and ideas about social functions are left over from an era where they were necessary for social survival. They have persisted into an era in which they are no longer viable. The result can only be called severe role dysfunctionality for women."[10]

Because of this, both at work and at home we live with constant, unsettling feelings; guilt that we don't really deserve what we have, and fear of losing it if we aren't one hundred percent all the time. The reality is, in today's world, women are still bearing the brunt of relationship, childcare, and domestic responsibility. Here, terms are telling: a man who cares for his children is labeled Mr. Mom; when men do their share of housework, they're applauded for "helping." Even when men assume their rightful share, women may still feel responsible, as if they are shirking their duty, which they then make up for with compulsive house-cleaning, indulging their children, or feeling they must keep up a perfect appearance.

At work, women are especially prone to overcompensate in order to prove their worth. And for good reason. Although women make up nearly fifty percent of the work force today, our footing is still mighty shaky. We may be in the door, but we still lack total access to the corridors of power. So we push ourselves harder, apologetically grateful for the chance to earn what is already right-fully ours. We may have come a long way, but we've got a long way to go.

WHO'S KEEPING SCORE?

Competitiveness, a thread running through the very fabric of our society, plays a major role in the pressure to be perfect. For most of our formative years, we are graded in school, often on a curve, where achievement is measured by outcome, not effort. For girls, there is the double whammy of being taught that competition is unladylike, resulting in confusion and shame over our desire to stand out.

Women compete with other women for men, for jobs, for friendship; we compete over whose child is best-looking and most remarkable. We are competitive in our efforts to accomplish (Who can get the most done without collapsing?) and even in our lowest moments (Who has the sorriest tale to tell?). Rather than encour-age other women to accept themselves, we spur each other on in our drive to be indispensable, to be perfect.

More than anything else, we have learned to compete with *ourselves*. Having been raised on competition, we've each got a running internal scoreboard that acts as a constant reminder that we're never ahead.

It's impossible to escape the messages inherent in our socialization. When we were children, they whirled around like a cyclone, sweeping us up in their path. Now, as grown women, we must recognize them, in the hopes of transcending them.

MEDIA AND
ADVERTISING
IMAGES
▼

The composite image of what makes an attractive, successful woman—complete with products and promises to achieve such status—is largely traceable to the flood of advertising we are constantly exposed to. The media, particularly television, is so much a part of our experience, we are practically oblivious to its impact. In the average American home, the TV set is on for nearly half of all waking hours, its hum a steady backdrop.[11]

Through both programming and advertising we are given powerful suggestions of what it takes to be happy. Most of us were raised on sitcom images of perfection: half-hour glimpses of all-American families couched in middle-class comfort, any conflict resolved with the perennial happy ending. In between, commercials showing marriages rescued by the sudden appearance of a perfectly executed stuffing side-dish gave the impression that anything is possible—indeed, all is within reach.

Network television, radio, and mainstream magazines are kept in business through advertising revenues, which are dependent on product sales. In order for a product to do well, the advertiser must first establish a need by convincing the consumer of how it will benefit her.

The majority of products advertised are targeted at women. Consequently, women are on the receiving end of slick advertising campaigns that promote the Ideal Life and highlight ways in which we are inadequate or lacking. Through billboards, commercials, and print advertising, we're continually assaulted with the message "You're not quite up to par, but with a little help from us . . ." The underlying assumption is that reality—dirty floors, dry hair, lifeless casseroles, and lackluster marriages—can be transformed into the ideal, or, beautifully kept homes, bouncy, gleaming tresses, gourmet entrees, and romance, sizzle, and sex, *if* the consumer recognizes her need for improvement and remedies it with what's being sold.

The pressure to be perfect is reinforced again and again in commercials that imply, subtly or blatantly, that it's the woman who's responsible for fixing anything and everything that's wrong with herself and her family. In *The Language of Advertising,* authors Vestergaard and Schroder explain, "Happy family adverts all imply that if the female reader's everyday life isn't as happy and harmonious as that portrayed in the advert, the shortcomings are in some way due to her inadequacy in fulfilling the functions required of a good wife and mother. The problems of the family, frequently socially determined, are thus individualized, and incipient despair is converted into a consumption-directed effort, which is allegedly capable of reinstating the agreement between the ideal image and experienced life."[12]

The "ideal" as fostered by media and advertising is primarily focused in two areas: first, physical beauty and sex appeal; and second, the image of the perfect wife, mother, and housekeeper, happily absorbed in making sure her family is getting what they need.

It doesn't take more than five minutes watching network television or flipping through a magazine to see what our society considers the ideal of feminine beauty: wrinkle-free and model-thin for starters. The overwhelming majority of television personalities, actresses, and models, rather than resembling healthy, run-of-the-mill people, conform to this ideal, which feeds into our feelings of insecurity. And once the consumer's feelings of inadequacy are tapped, products are presented as if they contain the miracle cure.

In the United States, $1.1 billion are spent annually advertising toiletries and cosmetics, another $417 million on apparel, footwear, and accessories. An average of fifteen new beauty products are introduced into the market each week.[13]

Christie Brinkley, the consummate all-American model, shimmies and shakes her billows of long, blond hair, promoting a well-known brand of shampoo. The subliminal message: Two capfuls and you, too, might look like a cover girl. A Maybelline eyeliner commercial promises, "Wearing it is a matter of perfecting your tone." Consider the perfume ad of a woman wearing only a strand of pearls topped with the seductively off-hand caption, "Notice anything new, dear?" The implication is that just a touch of this expensive fragrance promises the luxury of pearls and an attendant male to admire them.

The pressure to be a sexy partner, smoothly manage the housework, raise happy, beautiful children, and be a career dynamo without so much as a hair out of place, is fostered by media images. Although we are seeing an increasing number of more realistic female characters, especially on nighttime network television, overall the media both mirrors and perpetuates the myth of "Superwoman." Female characters in afternoon soap operas are dressed as if they're waiting for the limo to take them to a cocktail party, even when they're hanging out having coffee and schmoozing. Apparently none of the women in Pine Valley wash dishes, change sheets, or make dinner, judging by the way they're dressed.

While commercials pushing the image of woman in an exclusively domestic role have certainly decreased, they have far from disappeared. The majority of ads for household products are still directed at women and show satisfied consumers demonstrating them or lauding their remarkable features. One commercial shows three older women, who seem just a little bit wacky, singing the praises of Murphy Oil Soap while scrubbing down the pews and altar of an empty church. They appear ecstatic to be engaged in this pursuit of cleanliness. A male narrator comments on how "thrilled" the ladies are by the results, and vows, "If it's good enough to clean 'this house,' it's surely good enough to clean yours." A commercial for Palmolive dish soap shows several different women throwing and breaking dishes and glasswear in outrage at the residual spots.

These and numerous other advertisements continue to promote the image of woman as perfectionistic domestic servant and nurturer, despite the fact that for most women, housework comes at the end of a long list of other demands, and at the end of an exhausting day.

As the contemporary American woman has taken on more diverse responsibilities, advertising's response is to come up with products and pitches to ease the multiple-load of mother/house-wife/lover/breadwinner. Instead of providing examples of women making choices and finding ways to balance their roles—like asking for help—the pressure is on to tough it out, whatever the price. Of course, media role models would have us believe that juggling family and work is a snap. And when it isn't, it's long-suffering women who continually excuse men and children and willingly pick up the slack, nine times out of ten, with a smile.

TV moms are frequently depicted as totally selfless and with all sorts of help at their fingertips. In one commercial for Coast soap, a bleary-eyed young mother drags herself out of bed, trips over several toys strewn about the floor, wearily inventories the previous day's damage, and with a look of desperation asks, "Do I *have* to be a mom today?" Next frame: We see her in the shower, luxuriously lathering herself, smiling happily. Next frame: Rested and refreshed, the woman is engrossed in a game of touch football with her children. She looks into the camera and says, "I'm just getting started." Apparently a bar of soap has erased all her problems. In another commercial, we see a spanking-clean floor that Mom has just cleaned. In rushes her son, half the neighborhood in tow, looking for the beverage being advertised to dole out to his friends, and tracking mud across the floor. When the mess is pointed out by one of the children, our heroine's son says, "Don't worry, my mom doesn't care." In the voice-over, Mom tells us, "He's wrong. I *do* care." She's so thrilled her son has chosen this nutritious product, what difference if she has to start all over on the floor? The clear message: Good mothers put their children's needs ahead of their own.

One way the media has addressed women's multiplying pressures is by glamorizing the image of the Superwoman. A full-page perfume ad in *Cosmopolitan* reads, "Lady . . . you're free! Country proud. Playing in the big leagues. You're so busy taking care of everybody else. Who's going to take care of you? You! You're an American phenomenon. With a new fragrance all your own. All American. LADY STETSON. Every other woman in the world wishes she were you." Another ad, run in several national magazines, shows a woman's profile staring up at a gorgeous gold band. The copy reads: "Smart . . . just the right look for Monday's meeting. What a great way to break through all those pinstripes. Gold's terrific." Then, in italics, "Whatever your role, from editor-in-chief to mommy, you can always find the right design in real gold to express it."

Because our society is so oriented toward consumerism, we are easily convinced we can't live without this or that product. Even as intelligent adults and discriminating consumers, we are vulnerable to the suggestion that carrying a gold card or sporting a European-made stroller elevates our status. We want to believe— need to believe—that we can be happier, prettier, richer, and more popular if we buy a particular product.

Given the rigors of day-to-day life, we are hungry for even momentary escape. But in childhood, when these messages are first inculcated, the powers of discernment necessary to separate fantasy from reality are missing entirely.

I have witnessed my preschool children entranced with Saturday morning commercials for all manner of frivolous items. One particularly pernicious scenario shows a small boy, new to the neighborhood, sitting all alone on the school bus. He clutches his stuffed bear, built-in tape recorder nestled within its tummy. First frame: The boy pathetically contemplates the long lonely ride. He reaches over and pushes the bear's belly button. Next frame: Instant popularity as the children jostle for the favored position of best friend to the new boy *and*, of course, his teddy bear, which happens to retail for just under sixty dollars.

One reason media images carry so much weight is that they operate on both direct and subliminal levels, aimed at penetrating the subconscious so as to influence our buying decisions. As we distractedly flip through the pages of a magazine, we begin to wish for things we didn't even know existed. Having stared at fashion spreads of beautiful women in gorgeous apparel for so many years, it's no wonder most women are dissatisfied with their appearance. Just as the housewife of the fifties bought the idea that happiness could be had for the price of a nifty appliance, the nineties' woman aspires to bionic images of integration: motherhood, career, and romance rolled into one.

The media clearly plays an active role in influencing our struggles to come to terms with our flaws and limitations, with the fact that our lives usually bear greater resemblance to the overstressed, disheveled woman on the commercial for Extra-Strength Tylenol than the one whose spray deodorant lasts until she sweeps into her lavish penthouse after an exciting night at the disco. The repetition of peppy jingles promising nirvana by way of toothpaste and sixty-second flashes of cars with mythological names descending onto mountaintops create deep grooves and impressions, making it hard to sort out what's underneath our need to *have it all and be it all*.

Consider what part the media has played in creating your expectations of yourself. What television programs, radio personalities, commercials, billboards, and magazine spreads have helped form your idea of the good life? As ingrained as these images are, simply being conscious of them begins to reduce their hold.

OF VIRGINS
AND MARTYRS

▼

Religion teaches us how to be "good." The very goal of organized religion is to establish a moral, ethical code and instill the conditions for righteousness, and ultimately, for salvation. Our religious conditioning has a powerful impact on the roots of perfectionism and indispensability.

Western patriarchal religion sets up a parent-child relationship in which God is perceived as absolute judge of our behavior, master of our destiny. A thirty-six-year-old woman who hasn't been to church in fifteen years says, "I have only to close my eyes to recall the flowing white beard and Yoda-like visage of the imaginary God of my childhood. My personification of God was that He was all-knowing, which could only mean He knew exactly what I was up to even if I was hiding under the bed or going to the bathroom. If I ever in my life wanted to be good, it was on the day I heard the rumor He was everywhere at once, always watching." This image is shared by many women, most of whom had similar experiences growing up in a predominantly Judeo-Christian culture.

Religious doctrine provides a prescription, but it is the dramatic and colorful biblical characters that serve as example and inspiration. The theme of woman split as madonna/evil temptress/ martyr is present throughout Judeo-Christian thought. As young girls, we were drawn to images of the sanctity of the long-suffering Blessed Virgin Mary. Jewish foremothers like Sarah and Rebecca are similarly revered for acts of self-sacrifice and service.

The conditioning to be martyrlike has deep roots in biblical scriptures. For starters, in Genesis, we are told that God created Adam, and out of Adam's rib, a helpmate was created—Eve. Right off, it's clear that Eve, representing Everywoman, stands second in line. She isn't afforded full individual worth; her existence is seen only in relation to Adam.

Woman's status further deteriorates in the Creation story when Eve, eating of the forbidden fruit and seducing Adam to join her, is held responsible for the Fall from grace. The way the story is told, while both feasted in the garden, Adam is the passive victim—the onus for original sin is on Eve. Author Bernard P. Prusak, in the article "Woman: Seductive Siren and Source of Sin," explains, "Authors in a patriarchal society killed two birds with one stone. They explained the de facto existence of evil by indicting woman as its source and thereby also had both a theological explanation and the justification for maintaining the cultural facts of male domination and female subservience."[14] The Creation story clearly establishes woman as bearing the burden for sinfulness, one heavy mistake for the female psyche to continually atone for. Eve, as the first female role model, helps account for why women are more vulnerable to feeling inherently "bad" and looking for ways to redeem themselves.

For women raised in either Judaism or Christianity, the "good" woman, one worthy of praise and redemption, has been described as one who devotes herself to servicing the needs of her family. According to the Talmud (the sixty-three-volume explanation and interpretation of the Torah, the Five Books of Moses), the role of woman is strictly defined within the home. A woman was "chattel," a possession to be handed over from her father to her husband. According to the ketubah, the legal marriage contract, the man was to provide for the woman's full support; in exchange, it was her job to have children, make a comfortable home, and tend to her husband's personal needs. When she married, all of a woman's assets were assumed by her husband, leaving her completely dependent on his support.

In Jewish life, woman's role as nurturer has always been a mixed blessing. Dating back to the destruction of the Temple, when the home became the focal point of Jewish life, women were revered because the home was their domain. Alas, just one more gilded cage. Maybe they ran the show at home, but, at the same time, women were excluded from the highest pursuit of Judaism—the opportunity to study.

In her article "Images of Women in the Talmud," Judith

Hauptman says, "We can conclude that a woman's role in life is only supportive, that a man whose life is devoted to the worship of God, study, and productive, meaningful work outside the home cannot achieve these goals unless a woman stays at home to care for him and his children. In short, a woman's mind and energies are to be directed to fulfilling a man's needs, so that a man's mind and energies can be directed to fulfilling the broader needs of God and man."[15]

These attitudes are further reflected in the discrepancy between the number of commandments men and women are expected to obey; according to the Talmud, men are obligated to observe 613 mitzvoth (good deeds) while women are only expected to observe seven. The reason is, women are excluded from time-bound commandments because "if a woman who was occupied with child rearing and caring for her husband and home was obligated to fulfill all the commandments, she would find that religious and familial obligations made conflicting demands."[16]

Women don't fare any better in Christianity, especially in fundamentalist circles, where the family is structured so the man represents God, and is thus considered the "head" of the family, whereas the woman symbolizes the temple, God's home on earth. Paul, on the one hand, declared: "There is neither Jew nor Greek, there is neither slave nor free, there is neither male nor female; for you are all one in Jesus Christ" (Gal. 3:28). Yet he also preached: "Women, serve your husbands," (Eph. 5:22) and "For a man ought not to cover his head, since he is the image and glory of God; but woman is the glory of man" (1 Cor. 11:7) and "As in all the churches of the saints, the women should keep silence in the churches. For they are not permitted to speak, but should be subordinate, as the law says" (1 Cor. 14:33–34).

The power of religious indoctrination comes in part from its mystical undercurrents. In childhood, where they are first introduced, fantastic tales of miracles are used both to illustrate and intimidate. To our less educated ancestors, lacking the advantage of scientific explanation, an eclipse of the sun was grist for religious conversion. Likewise, to a child, awesome stories of deep seas parting and loaves multiplying are motivation enough to heed the word and follow the path.

For many young women, sometimes continuing into maturity, religion taps a fervent wish to reach for a higher place within ourselves. The hushed reverence of a house of worship and passionate sermons on the meaning of life arouse the desire to strive for goodness and grace. We are all, in our own way, looking for answers. But instead of serving as a guidepost on a spiritual journey, religion becomes a stern taskmaster.

The feminist play *Haunted by the Holy Ghost,* by Jan Magrane,[17] deals with the emotional implications of being raised in the Catholic church. The playwright told me: "Most women who grew up Catholic trace their perfectionism directly to their religious upbringing. In the Catholic church there is a duality between heaven and hell; good and evil. According to Catholicism, we come into the world with original sin, which in our child's-eye view, is like having a big black mark on our souls. Once it is removed through baptism, we become immersed in trying to keep our souls clean, by censoring 'bad' thoughts, going to weekly confession, even keeping a sin diary. We end up obsessed with our own goodness and badness, our budding sexuality mirrored against the purity of nuns, armpits and genitals cloaked within the folds of immaculate black and white robes, and the ultimate role model, the Blessed Virgin Mary. The only way to be good is to be perfect."

Once again, we must discern between trying to fulfill our potential and striving for perfection. In the same way that we have been conditioned to feel we must earn our parents' love, our teachers' approval, our mate's support, women have been inculcated to believe we must work to be saved. Instead of believing, really knowing, we are good, we grasp a formula for salvation. The implication is that we are inherently bad, a perversion of God's intentions. According to the Reverend Canon Rona Harding, a high-spirited Episcopal priest, "Christianity teaches that we are good, valuable human beings. Scripture says, God created Adam and Eve, and it was good. Yet we seem to be more comfortable believing something is wrong. That there must be something to do to *earn* salvation. We get hooked into anything that tells us how to be good, instead of accepting that we already are. The concept of salvation through works is deeply appealing to the human psyche."

And if God in all His perfection is the ideal, we certainly have our work cut out for us. A few years back during the Jewish High Holy Days, I was struck by a sermon Rabbi Stephen Pinsky gave about the meaning of the word "sin." He explained that in Hebrew, the literal translation is "missing the mark," and so sin, which we usually associate with failure or shame, is really noble effort gone awry. What could be easier to accept? Or more human? There is, after all, a distinction between humanness and godliness. Or as one person succinctly phrased it, "There are only two things you need to know about God: God exists. And you're not her."

If the pronoun "her" used in conjunction with God seems foreign, it is because the language and symbols of western religion are almost exclusively male. For anyone, trying to measure up to the image of God, in all His perfection, is impossible. For women, perceiving God as male, it is doubly difficult to identify ourselves as holy and God-like and good.

While women are gradually entering the heretofore closed ranks of religious leaders, most of us were raised within communities where women were nuns, men priests, ministers, or rabbis. We learned that spiritual greatness is a masculine realm and that women are the supporting players. Like the heroines missing from the pages of our history books, images of female warriors, priestesses, and goddesses are sorely lacking from our patriarchal religious heritage.

It is essential to embrace, create, and worship female images of goodness and power, so as to celebrate our spirituality rather than be at odds with it. It is imperative to stretch the meaning of spirituality, and with it, the narrow definitions of male and female, so that human potential can be aided rather than inhibited by religious lessons. Most important, we must begin by believing we were put here on purpose, and accept that we are good, by virtue of being part of creation.

RE-CREATING
THE CONDITIONS
▼

Over a lifetime of being told your self-worth is conditional, you begin to believe it. Initially, you absorb messages from the external forces informing your reality. In time, they are internalized into expectations. You re-create the conditions, building them into the very structure of your life.

As long as we see our self-worth, our validity as persons in terms of conditions and qualifications, loving ourselves for our achievements instead of our essence, we remain entrenched in a self-destructive pattern. If we believe we are lovable because of what we *do* rather than who we *are,* we keep creating new conditions that are impossible to meet.

How far do we have to go to convince ourselves that our best is enough? How long are the first three feet of infinity?

Like any other learned behavior, we hang on to making ourselves indispensable because it has served us in the past. We continue to get something out of it. So we continue to do it.

FIVE

PAYOFFS

Understanding your conditioning, how the various forces in your life have shaped you, provides insight into the past. But it doesn't necessarily account for choices in the present.

You may not be aware of how you are meeting your own needs by making yourself indispensable. You may think your schedule is overloaded because of others' incompetence or insensitivity, rather than seeing how you pile more on because you want to be appreciated and needed. Some women complain of too much stress, but can't see how they get a thrill out of handling more than seems humanly possible. Or fail to recognize how their need for drama is met by accepting crushing responsibility. Convinced that without their energy, attention, and orchestration, important details will be neglected or missed altogether, they push on relentlessly.

It's difficult to form an accurate picture of yourself when you're all caught up in activity. In your mind, there's no question you *are* indispensable—not because you want to be, but because you *have to be*. Have you considered what you're *getting* out of the bargain?

PERFECTIONISM
IS HABIT-FORMING

As we saw in Chapter Four, the patterns we play out as adults originate in childhood. Over time, you develop a pattern of being a "do-gooder" and "people-pleaser" because it seems to work. And so you keep doing it and doing it, until it becomes a habit, something that is part of your identity.

Habits develop slowly, gradually, over a long time. Little by little, our habits become so familiar, so much a part of who we are, that they feel like a second skin. The more habitual the behavior, the more difficult it is to modify.

Change isn't easy for anyone. We are most comfortable and secure with what we know. Even when our choices cause us pain, the thought of trading them for an unknown quantity is enough to make most people run quickly back to what they can count on.

Apathy and laziness are also factors in resisting change. Underneath apathy is hopelessness; we fear our chances of improving our circumstances are slim to none. In *The Road Less Traveled*, author M. Scott Peck writes, "A major form that laziness takes is fear. Much of our fear is fear of a change in the status quo, a fear that we may lose what we have if we venture forth from where we are now."[1] But what is there really to lose?

As with other addictive processes, in the early stages of making yourself indispensable your behavior serves as a coping mechanism. Perhaps as a child, unable to verbalize your hunger for praise and affection, you tried to please by acquiescing, running errands, doing anything you could to attract your parents' attention. In school, you tried to impress your teachers by offering to do special favors, having "right" answers, and excelling academically. During adolescence, you were everyone's confidante, always on hand with advice and sympathy in order to make friends and find sure footing among those who appeared to belong. You may or may not have been aware of these kinds of behavior as attempts to satisfy real needs.

I carry around a vivid memory of myself at two or three years old, eagerly assisting my mother as she completes her chores. She moves from room to room; I trail behind her like a young duckling parading behind the mother duck, my small hands all tangled up trying to tuck in the corners of the bedsheets and fold the laundry. When I finish one job, I eagerly ask for another. Each time I succeed, I look up, eyes shining with pride, awaiting her praise.

Each time our needs are gratified, our behavioral pattern is reinforced. Just as an alcoholic's first drink anesthetizes her anxiety and emptiness, leading her to take another and then another, when our indispensability is rewarded with words of praise, a show of approval or appreciation, our insecurity is briefly assuaged.

The more certain behavior pays off, the greater your investment in continuing it. Initially, the aim is to fulfill basic emotional needs, but as you are repeatedly compensated, you come to expect and depend on the rewards. Over time, your focus shifts from operating in a survival mode to satisfying your dependency. You become intent on recapturing the positive feelings generated by your indispensability. In short, you get hooked. Hooked on the "rush" of constant activity and achievement. Hooked on having everything under control. Hooked on the high of feeling important and needed.

What are the compensations, the rewards, the perks of perfectionism? For the Indispensable Woman, the payoffs are concentrated in the following three categories: ENHANCED SELF-IMAGE, SENSE OF SECURITY, and BEING IN CONTROL.

ENHANCED
SELF-IMAGE

"Self-image" or "self-concept" are the terms commonly used to describe the "set of beliefs and images we all have and hold to be true of ourselves."[2] Self-image continually evolves and changes. It is primarily influenced by a combination of how others see us and how we see ourselves.

Every experience you have contributes to your set of beliefs and images. Each time you master a skill or succeed at a previously untried challenge, you experience feelings of pride and accomplishment, especially if what you've done requires a real stretch, physically or mentally. This information is added to your existing set of beliefs, producing a revised version of what you currently hold true about yourself. For example, if your previous exercise regimen included little more than getting up and walking away from the table after a meal, but you've embarked on a bi-weekly course of conditioning and are sticking to it, your self-image expands and alters to take in the "new you." Or let's say you've never considered yourself a genius, but after months of diligent study, you've received higher marks than you thought possible, along with praise from your professor. Maybe you're smarter than you thought!

Any occasion of success helps build a positive self-image. Each time you complete a project, perfect a strategy, avoid a pitfall, achieve a goal, or triumph over a difficult challenge, your self-image is enhanced.

As important, how you view yourself is greatly affected by the messages conveyed by others, especially the people you respect or those having direct influence over your life. Beginning with your parents, you are given daily data regarding how you are perceived, which is integrated into your picture of yourself. No one lives in a vacuum, and we all, perfectionists in particular, are sensitive to negative signals such as disapproval and dislike, or positive reinforcement such as recognition and support.

SENSE OF SECURITY

The hunger for security is rooted in childhood and continues as one of the primary motivators of human behavior. True security is elusive, but can best be tapped from personal, inner sources rather than from the fickle outside world.

Behind the Indispensable Woman's facade is a desperate need for security, a motivation so powerful she knocks herself out, literally and figuratively, trying to create it. Her resulting good feelings derive from a variety of sources such as financial stability, intimate relationships, and the place she reserves for herself at the center of things. Always in demand, working her way up the career ladder and into the hearts of everyone she knows, the Indispensable Woman is paid back for her efforts by a sense of security.

BEING IN CONTROL

The third category of payoffs involves both the reality and illusion of *being in control*. Control is a way of trying to counter chaos with order. It takes shape in our attempts to create structure for our lives and to hold power over the lives of others.

The drive for control runs deep, and is tied up with self-image and sense of security. We want to feel as if we have a handle on the random events that might threaten us. Through competence and organization, women who make themselves indispensable are indeed able to exercise considerable control over themselves, their environment, and the people in their lives. We rest easier knowing that our closets are clean, our checkbooks are balanced, and our relationships are in some semblance of order.

But ultimately, we are not masters of our destiny. Rather than accept powerlessness in any area, the Indispensable Woman seeks to expand the realm of her control. The comfort of command over day-to-day occurrences is satisfying, but also kindles her desire for more.

Establishing a strong self-image, a sense of security and control are universal needs. These categories can be further broken down into more specific payoffs:

- ### The Thrill of Being Busy
- ### Physical Order
- ### Tangible Accomplishment
- ### Career Advancement
- ### Material Acquisition
- ### Economic Stability
- ### Being in Demand
- ### Flattery, Recognition, and Other Strokes
- ### Running the Show
- ### Intimacy and Romance
- ### Friendship
- ### Combating Powerlessness

Some rewards are concrete, while others fulfill essential emotional needs. For each payoff, there are primary and secondary benefits. Primary benefits refer to what you *get;* secondary benefits describe negative or unpleasant consequences you *avoid*. For example, in the case of RUNNING THE SHOW, being in charge and making all the decisions is a primary reward. A second benefit is not having to trust or depend on anyone else.

Certain payoffs are more attractive than others, depending on your individual background and personality. One person is motivated by money, another by recognition, still another by position or popularity.

THE THRILL
OF BEING BUSY
▼

One sure benefit of indispensability is that you can count on being busy. The thrill connected with having too much to do may not be immediately apparent. But consider the reverse scenario. Have you ever been ill, or at the end of a vacation that dragged on too long, or have you gone through a low-ebb period when you've barely had enough going to keep you interested, much less excited? Your energy wanes, you drag around and can't wait to get back into the swing of things.

Anyone with a healthy, productive life-style is used to functioning at a fairly active pace. Most individuals feel invigorated when busy; women who make themselves indispensable feel something's wrong unless they're going full throttle.

A young receptionist articulates the payoffs of being immersed in activity: "When I'm really busy, like when several phones are ringing at the same time and my boss wants something done immediately, I feel stimulated. And important. I can tell by how other people react to me they can see I'm someone whose time is worth a lot."

Constant, frenetic activity satisfies in several ways. When you're busy, especially if your energy is directed, the excitement of accomplishment keeps your adrenaline pumping. As long as you're moving you feel vital and alive. When you stop, you may feel let down, anxious, even frantic.

"I can't sit still for five minutes!" exclaims Miriam, a wiry forty-one-year-old woman who's worked as a travel agent for many years. "If there's a lull I find something to do, even if it's just filing or making coffee. And I can't understand how some people sit at home and stare at the television. Even if there's a good show on, I have to do bookwork or fold laundry while I watch. I guess I feel guilty unless I'm accomplishing something."

It's common for women to describe a feeling of loss associated with the absence of activity when resting or just being still. Being occupied makes us feel more complete; it is a way of ignoring the emptiness inside.

Being terribly busy also provides a way to put people at a distance. How dare a friend or husband interrupt to ask a question or venture an opinion when it's obvious he'd be getting in the way? Or worse, expect warmth or closeness when he can't even get your attention?

Finally, busyness serves as distraction, an excuse to avoid dealing with feelings and examining the substance of one's life. It's commonly believed that being busy is the best cure for unhappiness or hurt. However, constant activity can also be a way of masking pain. Busyness creates the sensation of being "filled up," but doesn't alone provide real nourishment.

PHYSICAL ORDER

The knowledge that everything is in its proper place comforts and pleases the Indispensable Woman. It's hard to relax if every dish isn't done or a birthday card is overdue. And organization is essential if everything is to get done quickly and efficiently.

Physical order also makes us feel more secure and in control of our environment. When there is structure in our living space or work surroundings, we feel most peaceful and comfortable with ourselves.

For most people, physical order means keeping their homes, their cars, or their workspaces reasonably tidy and clean. For women who make themselves indispensable, nothing less than perfect order will do. Which doesn't necessarily mean that you will achieve such perfection, only that you will worry a lot about it!

The need for control makes it almost impossible to allow anyone else to be responsible for maintaining the order. One sixty-year-old woman I interviewed cleans her house religiously *before* the cleaning service comes. She says, "I have to get everything organized just so, or they'd never know where to start. Besides, I wouldn't want them gossiping to anyone about my having a dirty house."

Nancy, a twenty-seven-year-old dispatcher at a trucking firm, told me, "If there's anything left undone at the end of the day, I can't stand it. I just keep thinking and thinking about the one pickup left unassigned or the orders I didn't have time to file." Other women satisfy their need for physical order by constantly rearranging their furniture or fussing with their children's clothing or hair, continually trying to find the perfect look they can live with.

In addition, a spotless kitchen floor or pristine appearance may appeal to an inner need for purity. Many women describe feeling tainted and contaminated when their environment is messy or things are not exactly in place. When physical order prevails, we are rewarded with a feeling of having been cleansed. Or as the well-worn expression goes, "Cleanliness is next to godliness."

TANGIBLE ACCOMPLISHMENT

▼

If there's one thing that sets the Indispensable Woman apart, it's the sheer volume of what she manages to get done. By virtue of being intensely motivated, she is able to achieve a great deal. Her accomplishments are many and varied, and are counted with satisfaction and pride.

Women overwhelmingly point to the *end result* as the single greatest reward of perfectionism. Whether it's workaholism, compulsive cleaning, or "shop 'til they drop," the priority is on what gets done, regardless of what it costs along the way.

"Of course I get tired," says Emily, when asked how she manages to keep her eyes open at work after staying up until two A.M. helping her husband with his résumé and potting geraniums to help raise money for her daughter's basketball team. "Sean's up for this terrific new job which I really want him to get," she explains. "And if I don't sell enough plants, Mary may not get her new uniform. The old ones are just awful!"

Tangible accomplishments operate on two levels. You get the payoff of the actual fruits of your labor: the dishes get washed, the cake gets baked, the lawn gets raked, the report gets finished, the Christmas shopping completed . . . the list goes on and on. There are also a number of emotional rewards.

When we survey the products of our hard work, it naturally makes us feel good about ourselves. Who doesn't take pride in a beautifully kept home or a well-executed meal requiring care and creativity? Who isn't satisfied when mastering a difficult work assignment or surpassing a past running record, especially when rewarded with a promotion or trophy?

Accomplishments provide proof of our competence, our intelligence, our specialness. Not only to ourselves, but to others. The more tangible the evidence, the more we can create a favorable impression. Displaying our achievements by showing, describing, or even complaining about what went into them, leads to being noticed and respected.

"Can you believe how Amy takes care of those kids all day and her house still looks perfect!" remarks one woman of her grown daughter.

"That's nothing compared to Megan's schedule," says her friend. "I stopped by her office the other day, and did you know, they just got a new account and now she's got three new clients this month, but that didn't stop her from putting on the most lavish dinner party the other night. She did the whole thing herself!"

Whether competing with others or with yourself, the admiration you get and the pride others take in you bolsters your self-image and makes you feel more secure.

CAREER ADVANCEMENT

The desire for career advancement is often the driving force behind women's indispensability in the workplace. In order to compensate for wage disparity and discrimination that has traditionally colored their experience, women feel they must work harder, longer, and more productively in order to secure their positions. The concrete compensations are job promotions, increased access, and higher pay. The emotional rewards include status, self-esteem, and financial independence.

The majority of women who are climbing the ladder, especially those in corporate settings, feel that unless they maintain an edge and perform perfectly, they risk losing their footing. "I feel like I'm walking a tightrope," says Carla, a thirty-three-year-old product manager for a Denver-based eyewear manufacturer and mother of an eighteen-month-old son. Carla's day begins before dawn, when she takes advantage of the peace and quiet to prepare all Timothy's meals for the day and get ready for work. At 7:15

the sitter arrives. Sometimes the sitter is with Timothy until past sundown, but on those days Carla rushes home at noon to feed him and sings a lullabye over the phone before bed.

"My husband and I considered delaying our family until my career was more secure, but I just didn't want to wait any longer," relates Carla. "If I can just stick it out another two years, I'll be in line for the position of regional manager, so it's worth it right now in order to gain the benefits that will come with moving up in the company."

Nan, aged thirty-four, whose social life has taken a back seat to her career as counselor at a clinic specializing in eating disorders, says she wishes her job wasn't quite so important, eclipsing all the other priorities in her life. "I know I can't expect to get all my needs met from my work, but I believe in it and I get a lot back," she says. "Sometimes I worry that I should branch out more, take an aerobics class or go to the singles group at church, but frankly, I'd hate to give up one second of the time I put into preparing or facilitating my groups."

Nan's dedication is rewarded by financial independence and personal gratification. But instead of developing other networks, she also satisfies her need for emotional connection through her co-workers and the people she counsels.

Making yourself indispensable in the workplace, while paying off in a number of appreciable ways, can also result in neglecting other, equally important parts of your life. The path to career advancement is usually marked with well-defined rewards all along the way. Other endeavors, such as intimate relationships or personal growth, are not as clearly marked and offer more elusive satisfaction.

MATERIAL ACQUISITION

▼

The accumulation of wealth, whether in the form of money or material possessions, is one of the most seductive payoffs of perfectionism. Having money or things reassures us of our worth, much in the same way that our accomplishments make us feel more secure.

The average individual in our society is virtually consumed with wanting to have more, in part because of the convenience and pleasure material possessions bring, but also because of what they represent.

The trappings of success are the measure by which the majority of people judge themselves and are a major factor in how others perceive them. Most people are motivated to compete on a material level, even if having the requisite income requires working excessively and not getting enough replenishment or rest. There's something about the Joneses that still makes us want to keep up.

Financial transactions also reward us with feelings of power. Pulling money out of a wallet or sliding the credit card across the counter in exchange for a purchase makes us feel potent.

The Indispensable Woman is no exception; in fact, because of her perfectionism she may be more fixated on collecting material goods, as proof of her status and success. The danger is, she may get trapped into thinking her indispensability is reasonable justification for maintaining the standard of living she's established. At this point, the need to acquire material possessions begins to take over her life, instead of enhancing it.

ECONOMIC
STABILITY

Economic stability is qualitatively different from material wealth. One involves the necessities, the other affords the extras.

According to current statistics from the Council of Economic Status for Women, fewer than one percent of women in this country have independent earnings of more than fifty thousand dollars a year; 13.5 percent exist beneath what is considered the subsistence level.[3] While a few women have access to great fortunes, the majority of wealth is earned or controlled by men. Women's salaries are nowhere near commensurate with their contribution.

Maintaining a decent standard of living is a major reason women make themselves indispensable in the workplace. In 1986, seventy-nine percent of couples in the United States required two incomes to qualify for a mortgage.[4] Just being able to keep up with the cost of living, not to mention the enormous expense of raising a family, makes most women's salaries mandatory, no longer the "pin" money of the past. Single women who are sole wage earners feel especially pressured to succeed in careers in order to support themselves. For married women, working outside the home may be the only means to having luxuries they couldn't otherwise afford.

Gretchen decided to go back to work after her second child was born. She holds a real estate license, a profession she says is perfect because the evening and weekend hours make it possible to take care of her children during the day.

Gretchen has been extremely successful; she was quickly hired by a good firm, emerged as one of the top sales people within a year, and in recent months earned more than her husband, a CPA for a large corporation. She loves working; however, her schedule doesn't include any time for relaxation. She and her husband play catch-up most of the time. "But it's worth it," she says. "I got sick of scrimping and scraping just to put good food on the table. Since

I started working, the money pressure is really off and we're saving for the down payment on a larger home."

Most women are willing to make sacrifices if they must, but less so when it comes to providing for their children. The more reliant a woman is on her mate for financial security, especially when there are children involved, the more likely she is to ingratiate and try to please. In my Expecting Change Workshops, pregnant women discuss feeling considerably more dependent on their mates than before they got pregnant. Women who previously felt quite confident of their own ability to earn a living, feel more vulnerable during pregnancy, which increases their fear of losing their economic security. The natural response is to hold tighter to the relationship by making themselves indispensable. The threat of single parenthood, an increasingly common arrangement, causes women to put out more than their share and to think twice about creating conflict.

One older woman I interviewed spoke poignantly of trying to be a "perfect wife" in exchange for material security. "I grew up assuming I'd get married and have children, and that my husband would support us," Harriet said. "I never went to college, and I worked for about a year as a secretary before I had my first baby, but I wouldn't begin to know how to go about getting a job now."

Harriet's husband, the owner of a printing company and a pillar of the community, provides a handsome living; they have a beautiful home in the suburbs, take two vacations a year, and both their daughters attend expensive Ivy League schools. Harriet describes the many compromises she has made over the years, saying, "Leon works hard and his business involves a lot of pressure. He can have a terrible temper, and yes, he takes it out on me, screaming and criticizing me. But look, what are my alternatives? What else could I do?"

Harriet feels trapped, like so many women of her generation who lack the education and experience necessary to support themselves. "Whenever my daughters complain about school," she says, "I tell them there's nothing more sacred than their education. My only wish is for them to never have to be financially dependent on anyone."

Both at work and at home, until sexism is wiped out, women will continue to feel they must protect their security by making themselves indispensable. Despite what we hear about women making it in the workplace, the alarming truth is that the wage gap between male and female earnings is almost exactly what it was fifty years ago.[5] While both men and women may be motivated to keep a relationship intact for financial reasons alone, when a couple breaks up, women almost always suffer worse consequences. According to Stanford sociologist Lenore Weitzman, quoted in *A Lesser Life,* just one year after divorce ex-husbands enjoy a forty-two percent increase in their standard of living. The ex-wives' standard of living falls seventy-three percent.[6] As long as these inequalities persist, women will do what it takes to secure the necessities and the comforts money buys.

BEING IN DEMAND

Once upon a time a full dance card was an important status symbol. Today it's a stuffed appointment book, one with so many dates crossed out it's impossible to decipher. And that's not all. You have two equally pressing deadlines . . . one friend on the phone while another is on call waiting . . . and your "significant other" complaining that the only significant time you've spent together of late has been occupied in trying to coordinate your schedules.

Setting up your work life or relationships so you are sought after helps you feel wanted and needed. An intense thirty-year-old woman whose talent with the violin had earned her a recording contract and a respectful following, described the hassle of so many people all wanting something from her. "I sometimes get deluged; then I feel resentful of how much everyone seems to need from me," Terri said. "I have four students, all very promising, and I get frequent calls from people requesting interviews, trying to set up benefits, or wanting me to hear their five-year-old prodigy. I can hardly open my mail without being interrupted by the phone."

On the surface, Terri appeared victimized. Yet when I suggested she hire a press agent, she found half a dozen reasons not to. "But you'd conserve your energy if you didn't talk to every single person who calls," I said. "Couldn't you at least invest in an answering machine?"

"Someone might hang up and not call back," she answered, revealing the real reason for her reluctance.

Being in demand vindicates painful memories of waiting to be chosen for the fourth-grade softball team, waiting for the phone to ring the week before a high-school dance. Few of us experienced the real security we're certain belonged to the team captain, senior class president, or homecoming queen. We still search for the feelings of self-importance that come from being popular and pursued. Even when it gets out of hand, when friends, co-workers, children, and lovers are all clamoring for time and attention, being in demand erects a barrier against being alone.

FLATTERY, RECOGNITION, AND OTHER STROKES

The Old Testament says a woman of valor is worth more than rubies. Most of us will settle for a compliment.

Everyone enjoys being on the receiving end of praise. And why not? It feels good to know other people think highly of us. Because women are so dependent on external validation, the words "Good job!" are music to our ears.

Indispensable Women are perfect candidates for positive reinforcement. We get lots of strokes for holding everything together.

Our accomplishments are a source of attention and envy. And our willingness to do for others is rewarded by verbal praise and shows of appreciation.

Positive reinforcement comes in many forms, some more subtle than others. Flattery and formal recognition are the most obvious way people express their regard. Admiration can also be communicated through a smile, warm hug, or other outward shows of affection. Your friends may reward you by seeking your company, co-workers by deferring to your judgment, your children by competing for your attention.

Backhanded compliments and envy are two other ways people show they're impressed. One particularly amusing backhanded compliment stands out in my mind from a few years back when I was at the height of my indispensability. That day, as always, I was running fast and furiously, trying to do an impossible number of things at once. I was double-parked, having left the draft for a new book proposal at a five-minute copier just long enough to run into a favorite children's clothing store to pick up a birthday gift for my nephew, Scott. As I frantically flipped through the merchandise, keeping one eye on the door for the meter maids who regularly traffic the area, the owner looked at me and said, "If I had so many exciting things going on in my life, I guess I'd look haggard too."

The aura of competence worn by women who make themselves indispensable is another quality that generates positive response. Most people admire the ability to be organized and efficient. Others consider it a relief not to have to worry about, be there for, or rescue the Indispensable Woman; she does just fine on her own.

Looking competent and self-sufficient is a way to take care of other people. If you keep your doubts and worries to yourself, your mate can count on you to concentrate on his needs; friends can lean on you instead of the other way around; your supervisor can concentrate on helping other employees who need it more. By not making waves, you are able to focus on other people's needs instead of attracting attention to your own.

"The more I put out, and the less I ask of anyone, the more they seem to like and want to be with me," declares Hannah, whose job in direct sales for a pharmaceutical company has her on the road for at least two weeks out of each month. "I used to slobber all over people, telling them my problems, but no one really cared, they were just interested in talking about themselves. Now, I ask lots of questions, and if the conversation turns to me, I make sure I point it in another direction. It's amazing how popular I've become!"

Much of our behavior as adults comes from deep cravings to satisfy the need for validation that never got met while growing up. The more we receive external information telling us we are "okay," the more likely we are to engage in behavior that will elicit this response.

RUNNING THE SHOW

I wish I had a dime for every time I've heard some form of the following sentiment expressed by women: "But I *have* to do everything myself. If I leave it up to anyone else, it won't be done exactly the way I want it."

It's a burden to have to take care of every single detail of every single situation without having anyone to help shoulder the load. On the other hand, there's a real bonus to doing it yourself—you get to do it *your* way.

"Back in elementary school, when we had to do group projects, like the time we made a papier-mâché volcano, I couldn't stand to just do my part," remembers Alyce, a hotel food and beverage director. "I'd bribe the other kids with candy I swiped from home so they'd do something else, and then I'd just finish it myself," she says. "I stayed after school a lot, but at least I didn't have to sit back and watch them ruin it."

It can be anguishing for perfectionists to have to trust others to be responsible for something they care about; learning to trust is part of recovery. Self-image is tied up with top performance, and their feelings of security are contingent on being able to control the finished product. As long as you're running the show, you get to impose your opinions, your values, your way of doing things. You have a specific idea of how the dishes should be stacked, which way the magazines should be arranged on the coffee table, how the agenda should run, or how you and your mate should interact. If you loosen your grip—by lowering your standards or letting others put in their two cents—you have every reason to worry the quality will suffer.

Then, too, by taking charge you keep the work quota up. To the Indispensable Woman, idle hands are the devil's instruments. "'Here comes the slave driver,' jokes my husband every weekend when I present him with his list of things to get done around the house," says Marilyn. "If he'd get off his butt and show some initiative, I wouldn't have to stand over him," she insists. "But," she adds, "I suppose sometimes I get a little carried away with telling him what to do and how to do it."

Another payoff on indispensability is that you get to be a martyr. When you run the show, you deprive others of their contribution; then you can feel free to resent them when you have to do everything yourself. If they *do* get involved, nothing they do is good enough, because it's not done *your* way.

One Sunday morning, I asked (note: asked!) Gary to clean up the kitchen while I ran some errands. When I returned a few hours later, the children were sleeping, Gary was sitting with his feet up, reading the paper, and the kitchen was spotless, except for one toy that he apparently hadn't spotted near the door. I, of course, promptly tripped over it.

"How can you sit there so smug and relaxed when I just about killed myself?" I raged, waving the matchbox car in his face. "If you cared about what you were doing, you'd have worked until you were finished," I added, trying to make a case for *my* way being the correct standard, the only acceptable standard.

Allowing others to share responsibilities requires accepting their standards and giving up sole control in exchange for lessening your stress. Of course the real trick is to feel comfortable about somebody else being in charge, a tall order for the Indispensable Woman.

INTIMACY AND ROMANCE

▼

Each of us, fundamentally, is separate and alone—a reality most people grapple with daily and find difficult to accept. In her superb book, *Necessary Losses,* author Judith Viorst says, "We love as soon as we learn to distinguish a separate 'you' and 'me.' Love is our attempt to assuage the terror and isolation of that separateness."[7] The need for closeness, for emotional and spiritual connection, for love, distinguishes human beings from all other species. Love inspires our best moments; without it, we experience loneliness and despair.

While she gives the impression of being exceedingly independent, no one longs for intimacy or fears aloneness as much as the Indispensable Woman. Her efforts to please are rooted in her struggle to ward off potential abandonment.

It is a sad truth that most individuals, lacking a fundamental trust in their own inherent value, feel they must *earn* love, rather than believing they are entitled to it. Perfectionists attempt to earn love by figuring out what other people want and then trying to fit the bill. They cultivate relationships in which they can feel needed and confuse that need with mutual commitment.

Sometimes it works. At least for a while, until one partner tires of the other or outgrows his dependency, which is exactly what happened between Jill and Rob.

When Jill and Rob collided on the slopes during a ski trip sponsored by their church singles group, the attraction was immediate and mutual. "I was blown away by Rob," recalls Jill. "He was gorgeous, and could charm the pants off anyone." The two were inseparable for the rest of the trip and began dating seriously when they got home. One year later they exchanged vows, returning to Montana for their honeymoon.

Soon after, Rob was fired from his sales job at a used car lot. The owner alleged Rob was moody, lazy, and unproductive, dreaming away his time while customers waited.

Out of work, Rob spent his days lying around the house watching television, except for the one or two times he went on job interviews. Many nights Jill came home to find him still in his bathrobe, unshaven, with his breakfast and lunch dishes in the sink. She'd try to build Rob up, clipping want ads on her lunch hour and giving him lots of encouragement.

Rob applied for unemployment compensation, saying he had been unfairly fired, but his claim was refused. After almost eight months out of work, their savings began to dwindle, although by this time, Rob had stopped even talking about looking for a job. Every once in a while Jill tentatively suggested he go to an employment agency. "They're just a bunch of vultures," was Rob's reply. Then he'd reach over and put his arms around her, saying, "No one understands me like you, babe," which was often a prelude to making love. Jill went to her parents for money.

One afternoon Jill came home early from work with a bad sore throat. She walked into the house, went straight to her room to get undressed, and there found Rob with another woman.

Despite her disillusionment, Jill didn't seriously consider divorce. Little by little she plied Rob for details of his affair; he'd met the woman at the car lot and they'd been carrying on ever since he left. Jill offered to go to a marriage counselor, to give up her job, to move to a different city, anything to keep their marriage intact. "I know it sounds crazy," she explained in retrospect, "but at the time I'd have given anything to be with Rob. When it was just the two of us, especially when his arms were wrapped around me, I felt totally safe, absolutely wanted."

Jill never did leave Rob. He finally ran off with the other woman, who had inherited a large sum when her father died, enough to support both her and Rob in style for a good long time.

Jill's behavior is typical of a pervasive condition described by author Robin Norwood as "women who love too much."[8] Loving too much, doing too much, giving too much without getting enough in return is one way women make themselves indispensable. The payoffs are affection, emotional and sexual intimacy, and a feeling of security that, unfortunately, lasts only as long as the relationship remains intact.

FRIENDSHIP

Romance isn't the only place where women invest too much love. Close, committed friendships, especially with other women, can rival the most ardent love affair.

We need friends on many different counts—for intimacy, company, acceptance, validation, unqualified, unquestioning loyalty, and support. Women understand and value the rare treasure of a good friend: someone you can count on to hang in there with you—when you're down or broke or crabby or in trouble—without rejecting, criticizing, or judging you; who is interested in the minute details of your life, even when she's heard them a million times before; who will sympathize and empathize when you're hurting, and be painfully honest when it's called for; someone you can let down your guard with and confide in, who's acquainted with the messier, less appealing parts of your personality, and not only accepts you, but is honored to be your friend. For many women, myself included, the bond with really close friends—certainly with a best friend—is a source of deepest trust and connection. Soul mates are carefully nurtured, fiercely protected.

Friends are our mirrors. We check things out with them—our choices, our values, our career negotiations, our mates, the color of the outfit we've handpicked for a special occasion. Many women consider friends "chosen family," extending the circle of kinship and making an express commitment to be consistently involved in personal matters, to share successes, and mark significant life passages. In our friendships, we get to improve upon our more turbulent relationships with family. We do this by creating "healthier" patterns and cultivating new, more appropriate images that jibe with present reality. We come into friendships with whatever selective past histories we care to divulge; with friends we can reveal—perhaps even discover—the very best in ourselves.

Friends are our social networks, our companions, our bridges in the community. For single women in particular, friends form an essential support system. Most women who are romantically involved insist they still couldn't get along without their friends. Judith Viorst writes, "In addition to helping us grow and giving us pleasure and providing aid and comfort, our intimate friends shelter us from loneliness. For although we are taught to strive for, and to value, self-sufficiency, and although there is doubtless—in all of us—an inner core of self we may never reveal—it matters to us enormously that we matter to others and that we are not alone."[9]

We expect an awful lot from our friends. And we hold ourselves to impossibly high standards in return. When it comes to friendship, the list women compose of their responsibilities is staggering. At the top of the list: A good friend is there when needed. Period. No matter what. This blanket statement translates into a hundred million selfless acts that good and loyal friends perform to demonstrate commitment and devotion. Unfortunately, "being there" often gets twisted into indispensability: never saying no. Or repeatedly supporting and rescuing friends involved in self-destructive behavior. Or consistently putting out more energy than the other person; being so attentive to their needs, we forget our own and end up feeling angry and resentful.

Holly, an otherwise assertive person, who has little trouble setting boundaries in her position as plant manager for a plastics company, finds her friendships to be a source of both tremendous comfort and considerable heartache. "I decided long ago that friends were the most important thing in the world," says Holly. "I live alone and my friends are who I really count on, both day-to-day and when something big is happening in my life. But because my friends are so important to me, I tend to go overboard trying to be supportive. My house has an open-door policy—a few of my closest friends have keys—and they know they are welcome at any hour of the day or night if they need me. The problem is, they need me a lot. Several times in the past few months I've gotten crisis calls in the middle of the night. I feel pressured when one of my friends wants something—it just seems impossible to get off the hook gracefully without feeling like I'm letting them down. Sometimes it gets a little out of hand. I get home from work and I'm tired and want some peace, and then the phone starts ringing and I don't always want to talk, but I don't want to be rude either."

Because Holly feels so dependent on her friends, she allows them to make too many demands on her time and energy. She feels obligated to give and give in return for their companionship.

Cecile, a thoughtful, perceptive thirty-four-year-old professor, looks at her need to be indispensable in friendships in a different light. She says, "Being the oldest of five girls, I grew up feeling terribly responsible for my sisters. I started babysitting for them when I was nine, and because my parents were so inadequate, I always felt like it was up to me to mediate and protect them. These feelings of responsibility, of wanting to provide validation and support, have extended into my relationships with women friends. I make myself indispensable by getting them to be dependent on me, which I do by giving advice, sharing insights, and really listening, which is something most women are starved for. For me, it is very compelling to have friends who need and depend on me for advice and wisdom and direction. It makes me feel powerful. In a world where women can't direct our own lives, we compensate by trying to direct other people's lives."

In some ways women are more apt to make themselves indispensable in friendships than in families or marriages. Different rules apply. We tend to be more careful of friendships, less likely to take them for granted. We shy away from confrontation, afraid of seeming critical, of hurting each other's feelings or appearing disloyal. We confuse co-dependence with unqualified love and support.

Paradoxically, while we claim to be most "ourselves" with our friends, we are much more apt to let our mates or our families see our beastly tempers, nasty, irrational acting-out, or petulant fits of insecurity. Even though our family or love relationships may be more emotionally loaded, they are also better defined and more circumscribed than friendships, and so we feel more secure. With our families, no matter how bad it gets, we take comfort in the notion they probably will never drop us and vice versa. With lovers and mates, we test the limits to see how far the commitment really goes.

Commitment between friends is muddier, less specific in its promises. Boundaries are fuzzier. Friendship feels more tentative, more fleeting, more fickle. If we don't continually earn the favor of our friends, they may leave and go away. Women who are married, have children, or are involved in committed romances, feel guilty turning down friends, concerned about seeming uncommitted because of time and energy constraints. Single women, who can't fall back on prior claims of mates or children, find it even harder to say no and put themselves first.

While we look to friends to support steps toward personal growth, when it comes to indispensability, friends can be part of the problem, instead of contributing to the solution. Women make themselves indispensable with friends because they get lots of encouragement to do so, and little support when they try to stop. Because the majority of women are conditioned to dependency relationships, it is difficult for them to see the pattern in each other. If anything, they are competitive and spur each other on in their perfectionism and need for indispensability. If a close friend begins to establish stricter boundaries or stops being quite so accessible, we feel anxious and indignant. With friends, because they are chosen for similar life-styles, politics, and values—especially with friends who go way back—change feels threatening.

But change is inevitable. When we stop making ourselves indispensable in friendships—when we stop trying to be perfect and risk being more honest and drawing lines when need be—the quality and nature of our relationships naturally change. It's not necessary to lose friends, only to develop more equal, balanced friendships in which commitment isn't defined as indiscriminate agreement, loyalty isn't expressed as oversolicitousness, love isn't counted by the number of crises endured. Friendships where, instead of acting as savior, parent, counselor, confessor, and trusted confidante, we are two whole people, coming together to share in and celebrate one another's experience and growth.

COMBATING POWERLESSNESS

▼

We all wish for the power to move, manipulate, and control the forces governing our lives. Small children believe they are in possession of magical powers. As we grow up, our exposure to life's realities—the miracle of birth, the inevitability of death, the natural disasters and human destruction that plague the planet— replaces our innocence with a grave knowledge of how uncertain life really is. We protect ourselves from this knowledge, keeping it locked somewhere in the back of our mind. Otherwise, we might become overwhelmed, unable to go on with our day-to-day existence.

Most of us become aware of our powerlessness when something happens to remind us of it. On January 28, 1986, I watched with horror as the televised launch of the Challenger space shuttle ended in flames, instantaneously killing eight astronauts, including the schoolteacher who had been specially chosen for the mission. Once I was able to move, I became consumed with making chicken soup from scratch for my family. I scrubbed and cleaned vegetables as if our lives depended on it.

It's natural to try to combat powerlessness with action. By taking control of a situation, we diminish our feelings of vulnerability. Taking action, especially when it results in tangible accomplishment that can be measured, positively reinforced, and preferably shared with others, makes us feel as if we make a difference, however small.

The catch is, there are some things we have the power to change, others that are totally out of our control. We can make chicken soup. We can grieve with the rest of the nation the loss of eight human beings. But we can't bring them back.

Indispensability is a way of denying the inevitable. What better way to fight against mortality than to be absolutely necessary and central to everyone else's existence?

We *are* able to exercise considerable control over certain aspects of our work life and physical surroundings. Perfectionism pays off in a feeling of personal empowerment; we embrace our accomplishments, holding them close as if an orderly environment or completed work assignment ensures against losing our grip on reality. Even when the end product isn't commensurate to the time and energy invested, the simple act of making an effort momentarily relieves feelings of powerlessness.

Regardless of our supreme efforts to manage the outcomes, life presents itself in surprising and unpredictable ways. While we rationally know that miracles are beyond our realm, Indispensable Women operate as if almost everything is indeed within our control. We scurry around, planning, making lists, certain that with enough strategizing and organizing, we can stack the odds in our favor. Then, *boom,* something unforeseen and unexplainable comes up, sending us into frenzied activity in the hope of preventing any further such incidents. Our attempts at intervention create a false sense of control.

Similarly, we delude ourselves into thinking that indispensability gives us license to control how other people act, think, and feel. As you become increasingly important in other people's lives, and as they become more and more dependent, they may begin tailoring their responses to suit you. Ultimately, no one person controls another. But being able to manipulate another human being's responses, even on a temporary basis, makes for power that is both dazzling and destructive.

The Indispensable Woman is addicted to perfection. Every payoff of her quest is like a drink or a hit, bringing her relief. Gradually, over time, she builds up a tolerance. Like the effects of any addictive substance or relationship, at first a relatively small dose is needed to make her feel good. She enjoys the warm feelings, then the euphoria produced by her perfectionism, and goes back for more. As the addiction progresses, she ups the dose, needing more and greater payoffs to get the same high. Finally, she hits a ceiling, begins to experience ill effects, and finds that although she tries and is even successful for intervals, she cannot stop her behavior.

The Johnson Institute in Minneapolis is world-famous for pioneering work in the field of chemical dependency treatment and for developing the Johnson Feeling Chart,[10] which illustrates the cycle of addiction, tolerance, and reward. Feeling high feels good. But the nature of addiction brings on a cycle of diminishing returns; the same amount that could once be depended on for a reward or "high" is now simply a "fix" that sustains a bottom-line level of functioning.

This woman's story says it all: "I had been ill for days with a particularly bad case of the flu. I couldn't walk I was so wiped out. My mother called and offered to pick up a prescription. I hung up, got myself out of bed, and literally crawled across the floor to pick up my kids' clothes and get them in the hamper."

"Couldn't you give yourself a break?" I asked her.

"That *was* giving myself a break. I can't stand it otherwise. Getting it done gets me out of pain."

THE
HIGH COST
OF
OVERCOMPETENCE

What terrible pain was this woman, LeAnn, trying to escape? What catastrophe threatened if yesterday's soiled clothing remained in a heap on the floor? What demons drove her to drag her feverish body across the room instead of staying in bed where she belonged?

Take away the object of any addiction and there is pain. We act compulsively in order to ameliorate the hurt, anxiety, fear, anger, and sadness inside. When the focus of the addiction is removed, whether it's alcohol, pills, food, sex, money, love, or, in the case of the Indispensable Woman, perfection, underlying problems surface. Problems that were there all along, going back to childhood. Problems that become increasingly serious through avoidance and neglect. Addictive behavior masks the problems by temporarily soothing feelings of distress.

A shrill, insistent cry and a new mother is awakened. It is the middle of the night, the fourth time in less than three hours. The baby, barely a week old, has already nursed, but needs the comfort and security of warm, loving arms. The baby's father begins to get up, saying, "You're so tired. Let me this time." "Go back to sleep," she says, and reaches for the baby.

In the shadowy, peaceful darkness, they sit curled together in the rocking chair, mother and child, enveloped in warmth and intimacy, each one a haven for the other. When the cries are lulled into soft even breathing, she continues to rock. In the morning, the woman is bleary-eyed. She complains of broken sleep and feels sorry for herself. But it is worth it. In the night, for those few brief moments she is wrapped in symbiotic bliss. She experiences relief from feeling trapped in a troubled marriage, which after only short years seems a lonelier place than being alone. For those moments she stops questioning her identity and wondering whether she really has anything to give. She escapes the excruciating isolation of going through a life-changing passage—pregnancy, birth, and new motherhood—and feeling as if no one really understands.

When she isn't holding or rocking or nursing or changing or otherwise tending the baby, the woman's anger and sadness and fear reappear, rolling over her like a threatening fog. Only when her attention is riveted on the baby, when she must summon her energy to be in charge, does the fog lift and the pain dissipate.

Like LeAnn, who crawled across the bedroom to pick up her children's clothing, the new mother uses her indispensability to "fix" her pain. She may not name it or she may only address it long enough to figure out how to dull it or make it disappear. She isn't interested in facing it head-on, investigating its origins, or doing anything constructive about it. She just wants the pain to go away. At any cost.

And there are costs. Like the heroic Dutch Boy, the Indispensable Woman has her finger in the dike, which keeps her from noticing the waters swirling around her feet. For a while.

When you engage in self-destructive behavior, treating yourself carelessly and neglecting your own needs, sooner or later you pay for it. There is no way to inflict physical and emotional abuse without suffering the consequences. For the Indispensable Woman, the costs are cumulative, serious, and utterly unavoidable.

It's easy to see the rewards of perfectionism. As has been pointed out, there's a lot to be gained from making yourself indispensable! But what negative results are lurking around the corner?

STOPPED
IN OUR TRACKS
▼

In our haste to get where we're going, we rarely have the wisdom or foresight to consider the effects of our actions. As a rule, people tend to avoid thinking about the "down side" or negative repercussions of our behavior. We are masters of denial, finding excuses for the strife in our relationships, for the nagging loneliness that plagues us, for the insistent headache that just won't go away.

We are so preoccupied with our goals and in such a rush to reach them that we are out of touch with everything else. Our rigid attachment to the end result makes it difficult to concentrate on anything other than our destination.

I remember being stopped for speeding several years back. I particularly recall the sick feeling in the pit of my stomach when I realized the flashing red lights and blaring siren were meant for me. I pulled over, my hands trembling while I dug in my purse for my driver's license, furious at being detained. "I'm sorry but I'm running terribly late for an appointment," I told the officer leaning against the side of my car.

"Lady," he replied, "at the rate you're going, you'll be lucky to get there in one piece."

We shy away from thinking about consequences in order to avoid confrontation with anything unpleasant or painful. We go to incredible lengths, ignoring signs of ill health and unhappiness, to protect a positive image of our lives. When faced with troubling symptoms, we rationalize them as coincidental misfortune or circumstantial snags.

We are shielded by our arrogance. We cling to the childlike belief that the world is a safe, happy place, that we are immune to hurt and impervious to danger. The knowledge of vulnerability is something preferably kept at bay. Instead, we assume nothing bad can possibly happen to us (bad things happen to other people!). We secretly imagine we will not be held accountable for our actions.

Women who make themselves indispensable have a built-in difficulty recognizing the costs of their behavior. Their frantic pace precludes the time and psychic space needed for self-examination. Accustomed to focusing their attention and energy outward, they're particularly oblivious to inner signs of distress. Their perfectionism functions as a barrier to admitting, even to themselves, that they aren't functioning well or that anything is lacking in their lives. More than once, I have heard women say they haven't the time to *think* about how they're doing, much less do anything about it. I say, they can't afford *not* to.

Problems are useful warning signals that some part of your life requires attention. In the same way that a toothache indicates the need to visit the dentist, signs of physical, emotional, or spiritual pain are a cue to slow down and take stock.

PREDICTABLE OUTCOMES

It is no accident that women who make themselves indispensable share a host of well-documented physical and emotional ailments.[1] The consequences of perfectionism, when manifested daily over a substantial period of time, are altogether predictable. As the addiction to perfection grows, there are a number of costs that can be anticipated. These are separated into six categories:

- Lowered Immunity and Physical Neglect
- Stress-Related Illness
- Reduced Coping and Effectiveness
- Eating Disorders and Substance Abuse
- Emotional Heartache
- Spiritual Disconnection

Even when confronted with the costs of making ourselves indispensable, we may still not see. That's because the fear of examining what's underneath our behavior is greater than the discomfort of living with the consequences. In other words, we choose the lesser of two evils, an effective strategy only as long as our defenses hold up. Once they start to erode, the costs come into focus. Let's turn back to LeAnn to see how her indispensability affected her health, her work, her relationships, and her self-image.

While somewhat embarrassed as she related the clothes-on-the-floor incident, LeAnn, a bright, attractive thirty-three-year-old woman working on a master's in art history, had a ready explanation: "You don't know my mother! She would have said something awful, or worse, she wouldn't have said anything, just picked them up and given me one of her looks, the disgusted kind that says, 'What's wrong with you that you can't even clean your house?' I just didn't have the energy to deal with *her* on top of everything else."

It was hard to imagine this vibrant woman groveling for her mother's approval. Teeming with confidence, LeAnn counted among her accomplishments two lovely children, a marriage to a man she both loved and respected, and several dear friends of some years' standing. Besides her graduate course work, LeAnn sat on the board of directors for a local theater company and was active in her community's literacy program.

Outward success notwithstanding, LeAnn's compulsion to have the house in perfect order before her mother arrived was one of many ways she kept up appearances so as to avoid any hint that her life wasn't one hundred percent okay. As far back as she could remember, LeAnn had tailored herself to satisfy her parents and keep the peace.

LeAnn's father was a noted physics professor. In his early thirties he had published a groundbreaking report, the impetus for his being made head of his department. A well-acknowledged "wunderkind," he was forgiven by most people for his eccentricities and occasional outbursts of temper.

At home, LeAnn's mother usually pandered to her husband's moodiness. At times he was warm and empathetic, paying rapt attention to his wife's long-winded stories of what had transpired during the day. Other times he would storm out of the house in a huff, disappearing for several hours at a stretch. His behavior with the children was equally unpredictable. LeAnn never knew when her father was going to gather her into his lap and tell her wonderful make-believe stories, and when she would be ignored or pushed away. The oldest of three children, LeAnn felt responsible not only for herself, but for protecting her younger sister and brother.

"I never knew what to expect," said LeAnn, her eyes clouded with a particularly painful memory. The whole family had looked forward to being special guests at a faculty tea in honor of her father's appointment. The day started out well. They were all dressed in their best clothes and LeAnn's father was in especially good spirits. He seemed to enjoy the attention and opportunity to show off his family.

On the way home, LeAnn's mother innocently mentioned how much she had enjoyed meeting Tom, another professor in the department.

"Half the students are smarter than he is," remarked her husband, turning to glare at her.

"I just thought he was nice," she repeated.

"Can't you tell the difference between an intelligent human being and an idiot?" he shouted in exasperation. The fight accelerated as they went into the house. LeAnn remembered crouching behind the stairway, terrified by her father's violence, witnessing a venomous exchange between parents who normally spoke little.

As a small child, she became convinced that if she could just be perfectly behaved, everyone would get along and they'd be a "normal family." Maybe she was too noisy or too much trouble, she reasoned. She tried to be well-behaved, but sometimes she forgot, and at those times, she could tell her father became more irritable. She stopped inviting friends over to play for fear of what they might see.

LeAnn fantasized herself to be the source of her parents' marital strife, but her father's bouts with temper went back several years, a reenactment of his own family system. Nothing she had done had caused his problem and there was nothing she could do to cure it.

Pleasing her mother seemed equally futile. As the years went by, her mother's unhappiness had become increasingly visible, her once soft features drawn and taut, her pain revealed in unpredictable outbursts. LeAnn became adept at fielding her biting criticism by being sympathetic, and when that didn't work, being helpful, and when that didn't work, just trying to stay out of firing range.

"I married Nick so I could cross the street," said LeAnn, ruefully looking back on her engagement at age twenty. "Getting married was the only acceptable way to escape." Yet LeAnn moved barely a mile from her parents' home and kept up frequent contact, having lunch with her mother on Saturdays and calling once a day just to catch up. She continued to seek her mother's approval, engaging her opinions of trivial details, such as what to serve for dinner, as well as important decisions such as whether to go back to college.

More important, LeAnn transferred the pattern of behavior she'd learned in her family into her adult relationships. Her professors were impressed by the quality of her work and commitment to the program, considering she was also a full-time wife and mother. She agreed to chair the annual fundraiser for the theater, which took countless hours to coordinate. Her house was the neighborhood watering hole for the seven- to nine-year-old set and the grown-up crowd on weekends. Her children, her husband, and her friends appreciated her and knew they could depend on her.

Unfortunately, the same wasn't true in reverse. It's possible, had LeAnn been open, that she would have found her friends and family could give back in some very worthwhile ways. But LeAnn wasn't able to ask. Having grown up in an environment in which she bore the brunt of self-absorbed and demanding parents, she only knew how to defend herself by taking care of other people. Acknowledging needs or expecting them to be met was unthinkable.

Which is why LeAnn continued to load her life beyond what she could reasonably handle, driving clear across town in the middle of a blizzard to drop off a paper at her professor's home so it wouldn't be late, and then stopping to pick up pizza and rent a video so the children wouldn't be disappointed about their school concert being postponed. LeAnn didn't think to dress warm that night (or most days); she rushed outside without gloves or a scarf. She didn't consider skipping the board meeting when she started sneezing, or take cold medicine, or make an appointment with the doctor when the cold got worse, or mention it to Nick when blood came up during a particularly violent coughing spell. LeAnn felt panicky for a minute, then brushed it aside. It was silly to worry. Besides, she had too much else to do.

LOWERED IMMUNITY AND PHYSICAL NEGLECT

▼

The Indispensable Woman lives as if immortality were fact, not fairy tale. Actually, she is particularly vulnerable to illness, much of which she brings on through continual neglect and her always-on-the-go style. LeAnn's story is typical of women for whom indispensability is an open invitation to health problems.

Chronic, debilitating headaches, the sort that sear through your temple and eyeballs during the day and pound incessantly at night, were my clue that things were out of balance in my own life. Not that the connection between my behavior and my headaches came easily. On the contrary, I spent months having my head examined by internists, neurologists, chiropractors, and even a rolfer, before reluctantly facing the truth: I was carrying the weight of the world on my shoulders and the pressure was giving me one awful headache!

As you throw yourself into your work, your children, your friendships, love affairs, or marriage, your own needs get shunted aside. Between trying to do everything perfectly (allowing no provisions for problems or needs that arise) and trying to get validation and love from those around you, your health gets put on the back burner. You grow out of touch with the internal messages communicated by your body and pay less and less attention to taking care of yourself.

The human body is dependent on sufficient doses of nourishment and rest. When we deprive ourselves, because we are too busy to eat, too anxious to sleep, too involved in taking care of everyone else's needs to pay attention to our own, we become less resilient and increasingly susceptible to illness. Once that happens, our bodies begin operating from a deficit.

We are negligent when it comes to maintaining a healthy diet and getting sufficient rest and exercise. Our mental health is equally ignored; outlets for relaxation and stress-release don't usually make the top-ten list in perfectionists' lives. When they do, they're seen as one more challenge; the goal is a perfect body or the fastest running time.

Every now and again, on the rare occasions when we treat ourselves to good, wholesome food or take an entire day off just for ourselves, the scales begin to tip. These brief lapses are like pouring a pitcher of water into a starving houseplant. Momentarily, its leaves perk up, but without a consistent diet they droop and wither.

Preventive medicine, including yearly checkups, dental appointments, Pap smears, and other health maintenance, is another area where the Indispensable Woman slacks off. Her excuse: not enough time; it will wait; or as one woman said, "Frankly, I was so wrapped up in how necessary I was to the running of my family and my business, I never imagined anything serious happening to me. I suppose I just didn't want to find out."

Being too busy, too pressured, too absorbed in important matters to worry about your health is shortsighted at best and, at worst, quite dangerous. Avoiding or trivializing physical signs of distress won't make them disappear. Ignored, the slight muscle cramps persist and become increasingly annoying. One morning, you lean over to tie your shoe and *snap*—your back is out. The cough left untreated develops into bronchitis or pneumonia. You had too much going on to deal with it before; now you're forced to lie low for a month.

By depriving your body and failing to get regular medical care, you sabotage yourself. As you become increasingly stressed, trying to do too much without replenishing your resources, your immunity weakens and your risk of illness increases. When, in fact, you do get sick, it's a highly unwelcome interruption, and as quickly as possible, you're back in the driver's seat.

You may notice signs of physical illness without attributing them to your drive to be indispensable. Although LeAnn didn't mention the blood to anyone, it had frightened her. She promised herself to cut back on smoking, but she just couldn't do it. Every so often she'd make a firm vow to quit altogether, but then she'd stay up late writing a paper, or attend a meeting where lots of people were smoking, or something would upset her and she'd reach for her pack. Smoking helped her curb her hunger. She usually skipped breakfast and grabbed food from vending machines while studying, instead of stopping for lunch. At night, even when she took the time to prepare a nice dinner, she'd mostly just pick at it, too anxious to eat. Sometimes she had trouble swallowing.

LeAnn started to have dizzy spells; when she reached for

something high up in her front hall closet, the room began to spin. Once she had to sit in her car on a parking ramp for almost ten minutes to steady herself enough to walk to a meeting. She'd heard low blood sugar might cause dizziness, so from that time on, she carried a Hershey bar in her purse, which she'd take bites of throughout the day.

Two months short of graduation, LeAnn was offered a teaching assistantship, which she accepted, although it meant staying up late grading papers and being in class two extra days a week. Her hairdresser had remarked on the dark circles under her eyes, and she accepted his suggestion to use a lighter base makeup.

STRESS-RELATED ILLNESS

▼

LeAnn's symptoms came from a combination of exhaustion, physical neglect, and stress. The most common physical complaints mentioned by women who make themselves indispensable are all stress-related. They are caused or aggravated by anxiety and pressure stemming from unrealized expectations. Typical stress-related symptoms include: fatigue, headaches, back pain, gastrointestinal problems, and chronic colds and flus.

Medical research is still in the process of determining what levels of stress are healthy, providing necessary stimulation, and at what point and in what ways stress pushes the body out of balance, making it more susceptible to illness. However, a connection is beginning to emerge. The potential to reduce symptoms of stress through relaxation techniques including biofeedback and massage has been repeatedly demonstrated.

In his book *Is It Worth Dying For?*, Dr. Robert Eliot, director of the CardioVascular Institute at Swedish Medical Center in Denver, says, "Stress occurs when there is a mismatch between expectations and reality."[2] No wonder perfectionism increases stress, given the distance between idealized standards and realistic accomplishments.

In an interview with Dr. Eliot, he outlined medical dangers, saying, "Women who are perfectionists often become what I call 'hot reactors.' This is an individual who is plugged into too many circuits and whose body is in mortal combat all the time. Her physiology resembles that of an air traffic controller in a storm with twenty planes trying to land at different runways." Eliot went on to say, "When early signs of physical stress aren't recognized, an individual stands a good chance of developing high blood pressure, which is a key factor in heart disease. Other serious consequences include elevation in blood cholesterol, colitis, ulcers, and an increased tendency toward eating disorders and other addictions."

Stress exaggerates already existing health problems. One woman's psoriasis flared up during an especially stressful period at work. She underwent ultraviolet treatments of such intensity she needed to wear dark glasses for several days. Other women develop a chronic ailment out of the blue; sometimes a variety of new and old problems all sprout up at once.

Sandra planned and executed all the arrangements for her own wedding, including baking the wedding cake for the reception to which 350 people were invited. After returning from a two-week honeymoon in Hawaii, where she spent most of her time writing thank-you notes, she came down with a strain of herpesvirus. The doctor's analysis: stress.

Sometimes we get sick because it's the only way to give ourselves permission to stop. Have you ever been under so much pressure that once things settle down you end up with a terrible cold or flu? Running so hard you run yourself down is a little like overloading your washing machine: first you hear a disturbing pounding noise. You run downstairs and see the machine shaking violently, then with one last valiant shudder, it comes to a grinding halt. Time to call Maytag.

Everyone experiences periods of needing to slow down and regroup. It's a way for the body and psyche to repair the constant battering sustained in the pressures of day-to-day life and restore balance and vitality. Illness provides an opportunity to let down emotionally. We get much-needed attention, sympathy, rest, and support, especially if our complaint is minor and short-lived.

When we're sick, we can allow ourselves to shut out the world. We get to curl up under warm covers with a good book, or lose ourselves in passive, mindless television watching, or just dream away the hours. For women, illness may be perceived as an acceptable form of weakness. Remember those heroines in Jane Austen novels who gracefully fainted or took to bed with a touch of neuralgia when life got to be too much? No modern woman would think of retreating in such a fashion.

In an essay that appeared in the "Hers" column of *The New York Times,* writer Norma Rosen tells of a woman with an extremely fast-track life-style who is violently accosted by another jogger during her ritual morning run. The woman narrowly escapes, but her schedule doesn't permit the time to physically or psychically heal.

> So she telephoned her husband at his office and asked him to report the event to the police because she had no time. Nor had she time for a therapist. That evening she received a dozen guests at her house for a prewedding dinner for her oldest son, his bride- and in-laws-to-be. At odd moments she ran upstairs to her bedroom, shut the door and sobbed, then washed her face and came down again. She decided that she would not—could not—change her schedule.[3]

We never learn what happens to the woman in Rosen's essay, although we can assume her inability to deal with what happened takes its toll. Ask anyone who's survived a personal crisis or trauma; they'll recall a period of extreme fatigue, depression, or physical illness following on its heels. Usually, the period of breakdown occurs *after* the immediate trauma has passed, when it's common for people to say, "I finally had time to collapse."

Dr. Joanne Rogin, clinical assistant professor in neurology, University of Minnesota, told me, "Migraine headaches have been found more frequently in women with Type A personalities. In many cases, the patient reports a particularly stressful time during which she functioned just fine. Once the pressure passes, she comes down with a full-blown migraine."

Perfectionists are in a continual coping-with-crisis mode, so instead of catching up with themselves and taking the necessary time to let down, their stress accumulates. No single bout of the flu, upset stomach, or private moment in tears seems especially out of the ordinary. However, the physical effects of indispensability are not isolated incidents. They add up.

Not all stress leads to illness and not all illness stems from stress. But where stress *is* involved, the symptoms are warning signs that by making yourself indispensable you may be making yourself sick.

In the past twenty years, stress-related illness in women has risen sharply. As the responsibilities in our lives become increasingly complex, women are emulating the hard-driving male model, which is linked to ulcers, heart attacks, and shorter life expectancy. At present, women account for *one* in every *five* cardiac patients, up from only *one* in *twenty-five* a little more than a decade ago.[4]

LeAnn didn't check out the clear warning signs she was getting, even when they started interfering with her routine. She had trouble concentrating and being organized. Her performance in the classroom started to slip and she was surprised at how hard she had to struggle with the demands of her new position as president of the theater board. For the first time, she found herself being forgetful. Somehow, her father's seventieth birthday came and went without her so much as sending a card. She missed a lunch date with the theater's artistic director and she was forty-five minutes late for an appointment with her dermatologist, although she swore she'd had it right on her calendar.

The strain began to show in other areas of LeAnn's life. Usually good-tempered, she was irritable, even impatient when anything unexpected was asked of her. One evening LeAnn decided it was a great time to clean the refrigerator since both kids were busy doing homework and Nick was out on business. She was up to her elbows throwing out pickles and half-eaten cartons of yogurt when her professor called to discuss her research proposal. Right then her daughter came barging into the room and slammed her math book on the table, screaming, "You said you'd help me! I have a test tomorrow!" The instant LeAnn hung up the phone she grabbed Becky furiously and said, "Don't you interrupt! That call was very important to me!" then burst into tears of frustration and remorse.

Every part of LeAnn's life showed strain as her coping mechanisms deteriorated. Where was her skill at juggling day-to-day demands and handling crisis with aplomb? Why was it taking all her energy just to keep track of the next thing on her list?

REDUCED COPING AND EFFECTIVENESS

Perfectionists develop finely honed coping skills as a matter of survival. As they attempt to handle more and more, their indispensability backfires and they begin to jeopardize the very qualities in themselves they count on most: being competent, efficient, and organized to a fault.

Reduced coping shows up in the following ways:

1. Trouble concentrating

2. Forgetfulness

3. Impatience

4. Mental confusion

5. Inability to set priorities

6. Decline in productivity

7. Sloppy, careless, and superficial performance

8. Reduced perceptiveness and insight

9. Poor logic and reasoning

10. Lack of perspective

Most women report that their performance, whether at work or at home, suffers when they're stretched too thin. Nothing gets their clear, undivided attention. Their thinking is disjointed and they're unable to stay on track. Decision-making is also affected. The Indispensable Woman, once a master problem-solver, now has trouble focusing, remembering details, setting priorities, or doing a thorough job.

Eleanor, age forty, was in her sixth year as principal of a Catholic girls' school. Her position required polished skills in problem solving and conflict resolution. She was accountable for staff supervision, financial operations, curriculum development, and community relations.

Eleanor's attachment to the school went way beyond professional interest. "No one has ever been more committed to her work than I was, but I just didn't know when to stop," she said. "Every one of those girls was like a daughter to me. I carried their problems around twenty-four hours a day until they dissolved into one big blur. I didn't see it coming, but after a while I couldn't think straight anymore. My responses weren't sharp and I wasn't able to be objective or diplomatic. When moderating an interfaith panel on birth control, I actually got into an argument with a guest panelist and embarrassed both of us!"

Eleanor's years of trying to be the "perfect principal" caught up with her. "It got so that if one more person asked me a question, my brain was simply going to explode," she recalls. Students and faculty alike sensed she was operating on a very short rope and began to avoid dealing with her.

Living in a state of constant tension makes you less able to cope emotionally. Instead of taking life in stride, you're impatient and unable to keep things in perspective. The little things that didn't used to bother you feel like major aggravations. When anything doesn't go exactly as planned, you become agitated, furious at life for disrupting your schedule. Previously, your grace-under-pressure and willingness to give made you the first one to be called upon in a crisis; now, you may overreact or resent the imposition.

As coping mechanisms weaken, you become increasingly desperate. One woman, struggling to hang on to some shred of her past ability to cope, said she felt as if she were "sinking in quicksand." Another described grasping at straws, bouncing from one coping mechanism to another. One day she'd work until two A.M., the next day she'd obsessively clean house or make long lists of high-priority projects.

The Indispensable Woman, lacking clarity, insight, and perspective, is unable to see that these are last-ditch attempts to regain some semblance of order. Her reduced perceptiveness, at a time she needs it most, makes it difficult to identify that she is in trouble.

People began remarking on LeAnn's dissipated appearance. Of course her mother had always found reason to criticize: either she looked too chubby or her hairstyle wasn't flattering or the outfit she had on just didn't *do* anything for her. LeAnn was used to tuning out her mother's comments. But now friends began to notice LeAnn's weight loss. Her clothes hung on her and her new makeup didn't entirely disguise the deepening dark circles. Her eight-year-old told her he thought she should eat more. Nick said he liked women thin but not *that* thin.

"I'm just so busy the weight's falling right off me!" was how LeAnn laughed off everyone's concern. Actually, she liked feeling lean and mean; it was her little secret that her weight had dropped to under 110, the least she'd weighed since junior high. That wasn't the only thing she was hiding. She'd also discovered that by taking laxatives at bedtime she was able to get rid of the bloated feeling that slowed her down in the morning. And she liked fitting into the size six jeans she'd found at a campus boutique.

In order to sustain her new figure, LeAnn lived on apples,

cottage cheese, and black coffee. She wasn't able to sleep well, what with drinking eight or ten cups of coffee per day; after several hours of battling insomnia, she'd get up and try to do some work. But she couldn't concentrate on only five hours of sleep, and one night she took a sleeping pill. Two days later she took another. And the following night, another.

EATING DISORDERS AND SUBSTANCE ABUSE

Perfectionism is a natural bridge into chemical dependency and eating disorders. Individuals with addictive personalities have a general tendency toward other areas of addictive behavior and substance abuse.

Dieting is tricky. It is, after all, a national pastime. The vast majority of women are sensitive to the ideal of thinness; svelte is synonymous with success. For perfectionists, unwilling to accept anything less than a mythic "perfect body," the drive to control their diet gets out of hand, often leading to serious eating disorders such as anorexia nervosa or bulimia.

Rhoda Weber is a Los Angeles therapist specializing in eating disorders. She states, "Women who make themselves indispensable are extremely vulnerable to developing eating disorders due to the combined inner pressures of trying to perfect their bodies and a tendency to subjugate their own needs. An eating disorder is a way to attempt to quell the personal appetites, drives, and needs that might prevent or interfere with a woman's ability to focus solely on taking care of others. She tries to stuff down, throw up, or starve away her needs.

"In general," Weber continues, "these women grew up in families where their needs weren't met by their parents. Instead, the tables were turned, with the children taking responsibility for fulfilling their parents' needs."

It's common for women to become engaged in dangerous cycles of starvation, bingeing, and purging in a desperate effort to become or stay "attractive." Having learned a pattern of self-denial as a means of getting love, the behaviors are transferred into romantic relationships. Women believe their only hope of finding a prospective mate or keeping an existing romance alive is by staying a size eight or having a perfectly flat tummy.

Compulsive eating disorders may lead to a number of extremely serious problems, including stomach ruptures, kidney failure, calcium loss, electrolyte imbalances, heart palpitation, respiratory problems, mental confusion, and depression. In an alarming number of cases, the outcome is death. The mortality rate is higher for anorexia nervosa than for any other psychiatric illness. According to a November 1985 Gallup poll, five million Americans suffer from bulimia; one in eight teenage girls have symptoms of anorexia; and one woman in six binges at least once a week.

The incidence of substance abuse is equally disturbing.[5] Women who make themselves indispensable are extremely susceptible to the "quick fix," whether it's smoking a cigarette, having a drink or a cup of coffee, or popping a pill. Getting wired helps them stay awake, keep going, and get more done. Instead of submitting to physical limitations, they create false energy and pump themselves up. Wine, marijuana, or a tranquilizer helps them come down and mellow out enough to shift gears from their hyper pace and get to sleep.

Dependence on addictive substances can also be a way to give yourself a "treat," something rare in the life of the Indispensable Woman. Perverse as it may sound, when I finally beat my two-pack-a-day habit, I grieved at no longer being able to reward myself with cigarettes. For fifteen years I'd given myself this special little gift, seven days a week, forty times a day, upping the frequency when I was especially needy or down, and now suddenly it was taken away. Part of my recovery from smoking involved learning to nurture myself in other, healthier ways.

* * *

We use nicotine, caffeine, chocolate (which contains caffeine), and mood-altering drugs for the same reasons that we engage in constant activity: to numb and detach ourselves from pain. One addiction reinforces the other.

In her aptly titled chapter "When One Addiction Feeds Another," Robin Norwood explains it well: "As long as we are bent on escaping ourselves and avoiding our pain, we stay sick. The harder we try and the more avenues of escape we pursue, the sicker we get as we compound addictions with obsessions. We eventually discover that our solutions have become our most serious problems."[6]

All members of a family are affected when any one individual has problems with stress-related illness, eating disorders, or substance abuse. LeAnn's husband, her children, even her hypercritical mother were becoming alarmed by the changes in her behavior and appearance. Her mother tried to help by suggesting she go to the doctor. When LeAnn snapped at her and told her it was none of her business, she backed off. Nick worried about how thin she looked and noticed how often she suggested they have a drink. He made one attempt at starting a conversation about it, but when she accused him of being a spoilsport, he dropped it and took the drink she offered him. Neither Nick nor LeAnn's mother was willing to rock the boat. Both were primary beneficiaries of LeAnn's addictiveness; although neither could have articulated it, they were accustomed to and dependent on the "goodies" of her indispensability. So when LeAnn said everything was okay, they were only too glad to believe it.

What Nick *didn't* know was how much he was putting at risk by enabling LeAnn. Their marriage was a traditional one: he supported the family; she took care of just about everything else. Before they were married, they'd agreed she would be responsible for meals, social arrangements, extended family relations, housework, and raising their children. Going back to school and her part-time job and volunteer work hadn't been discussed, although Nick seemed quite supportive of everything she was involved in, as long as she was there when he needed her.

Over the years, Nick had grown to need LeAnn in all sorts of ways. From the first time he saw her, performing in her sorority's spring talent show and pouring punch afterward, he was attracted to her energy and poise. Nothing seemed to get in LeAnn's way. She was eager to get along with Nick's friends and the many members of his Italian family. During his last year in law school she typed all his papers and coached him with practice questions while he was studying for the bar. Once he was out of school and practicing, she took over the books for his business, doing them on the weekends, and on the many nights he had to see clients late, she took care of the kids herself, bathed and put them to bed, and waited up to see him.

In the early years of their marriage, LeAnn was probably no different from any young woman wanting to please the man she loved. But as her indispensability grew, her attempts to please turned into a controlling need to take over.

Instead of being interested in Nick's work and offering feedback, she gave him advice, suggesting he get out of his fledgling firm and go to work for a large corporation so he'd make more money. When his mother called long-distance, hurt because Nick had been out of touch for almost a month, LeAnn lied, insisting he'd tried several times but the line was busy, pacifying her instead of handing Nick the phone. During the last grueling weeks of graduate school, she stomped around the kitchen muttering under her breath instead of asking Nick to help her with the meals or the housework or the kids. When she got up to clear the table at a family dinner celebrating her son's ninth birthday, her father remarked how exhausted she looked. "Let's you and me do it," he said to his son-in-law.

"Nick wouldn't know where the dishes go," interrupted LeAnn, getting up to do it herself.

Although Nick and LeAnn felt the strain between them, they were equally stuck on playing out the roles they'd established in their marriage. LeAnn said she wished Nick would take more interest in the kids, but when he got involved with them, LeAnn butted in with suggestions or helpful hints about their likes and dislikes, or arbitration if anyone got testy. A few times LeAnn started to complain about how pressured she felt, but when Nick suggested she quit her job at the university, she decided he just didn't understand.

Nick started coming home later and later; nights when he didn't have to work, he'd grab dinner on the way to the health club. The distance between them deepened, and except for one Saturday night after a romantic dinner and several drinks, they stopped making love. LeAnn didn't care. Most of the time she felt cold and withdrawn, and besides, she had much too much on her mind to worry about sex.

EMOTIONAL HEARTACHE

Women who make themselves indispensable do it for friendship, for closeness, for intimacy, most of all for love. What a sad irony that we destroy the very thing we need most. Intimacy becomes impossible as we armor ourselves in a shell of competence and urgent efficiency. We lose touch with our sexuality and our need to touch and be touched and held close. Our senses of humor, delight, and wonder edge away behind a cloud of dissatisfaction and resentment.

The quality of our relationships suffers as we become more controlling and less able to accept people as they are. We hold others up to the same standard of perfection we expect of ourselves. We give our friends, our lovers, our parents, our children, our mates the message that we are looking for something specific from them. We make it clear that without it they are lacking. We lose sight of the special qualities and gifts that attract us in the people we love. When they fail to measure up, we criticize and shame them for letting us down. Or we keep our mouths shut but follow around behind them—picking up their socks, polishing up their work, finishing their sentences because we can't stand that *they* aren't any closer to perfect than *we* are. Their imperfection is a persistent and irritating reminder of our own.

On the surface, our hostility comes from our "legitimate" resentment of having to do so much with so little support. "He'd let his pants lie there until they walked away," we complain indignantly. "Wouldn't you get pissed off if you'd have to initiate *every* single conversation about your relationship in twenty years?" is our self-righteous retort. And it's true. We do more than our share, usually with very little help from anyone. Of course, rarely, if ever, do we ask.

Taking care of the people in our lives to the extent that we encourage them to be dependent and irresponsible isn't really being loving at all. We think we're helping make their lives easier; actually we're stunting their growth. The woman who constantly follows behind her one-year-old, arms stretched out in case he falls, or does her children's homework, or covers for her co-worker when he's repeatedly late, or for her friend when she lies to her husband, or for her husband when he's rude to their friends at a party handicaps them so they will remain dependent on her.

Dr. Susan Bidwell, a clinical psychologist with the Metropolitan Clinic of Counseling in Minneapolis, treats women with classic symptoms of stress-related depression. She says, "Women who make themselves indispensable spread themselves too thin and forget to pay attention to their own needs. When they realize they've gotten the short end of the deal they feel ripped off and embittered. Usually, they cast blame everywhere else, without seeing their own part in it."

The quality of our relationships is also impaired by an obsession with productivity and performance. Spontaneity is lost as we occupy ourselves with itineraries and details and time-frames that we dare not deviate from. We care so much about what gets done, we forget that we are dealing with sensitive human beings, not machines.

I was struck by how a woman on a local television show described her symptoms of burnout. She said she could always tell she was getting a little "crispy around the edges" when she became more concerned with crossing things off her list than with people's feelings. It was time for this woman to "step back" when, instead of giving her daughter a hug and asking how her day went when she came home from school, she'd pounce on her with questions about her homework being done or whether she'd cleaned her room.

The Indispensable Woman isolates herself by shutting other people out. Refusing their efforts, being critical, and never letting anyone see how vulnerable she really is, she deprives them of their right to give. Sooner or later they stop offering and go away, if not physically, then emotionally. Others may admire, envy, and even fall in love with someone who appears to be perfect, but eventually they have a hard time finding much in common.

"I worked for three years in a small organization of thirty-five people. In that time, my father died and my husband was hospitalized for chemical dependency, but they never saw me cry," says Kathlyn in retrospect, after participating in group therapy for six months. "I discovered that by presenting myself as indispensable, always pretending to have it together, no one could relate to me," she recalls. "No one could compete and no one could get close. I had no flaws—no faults—no friends."

It takes a tremendous amount of energy to keep yourself tensed and protected so no one sees who you really are. Satisfying relationships require the willingness to expose both frailties and strengths, to give as well as to receive, to trust another human being with your fears, your fantasies, your hopes, and your dreams, in all their imperfection.

Had you asked, LeAnn would have said she had close friends, a loving family, and a very devoted husband. But she didn't trust them. Not when it came to telling anyone she'd failed her final exam. Her head was spinning so badly she couldn't remember half the material, though she'd studied all night. She didn't trust her best friend enough to confide that her weight had dropped to one hundred and she was worried, both about her own health and about where Nick was on the nights he came home late. She didn't trust Nick enough to tell him she'd gotten a prescription for sleeping pills and she was taking two every night and was beginning to wonder if she might have a problem. She didn't trust anyone, certainly not her friends, her family, or her husband—who all thought she had everything anyone could want—with the fact that she was scared, lonely, and didn't know what to do.

So LeAnn crawled across the room to pick up the clothes her children had left lying in a pile. That's where her mother found her two hours later, feverish and disheveled, lying sobbing on the floor.

During her week-long stay in the hospital for pneumonia and exhaustion, LeAnn met with the nutritionist and agreed to build up her strength by getting lots of rest and starting on a high-protein, high-calorie diet. She took the opportunity to quit smoking and, when she got home, flushed the sleeping pills down the toilet and didn't renew her prescription.

Nick and the children visited LeAnn in the hospital every day. When she first came home, she got lots of attention and encouragement. Nick cooked dinner and the kids applauded when she finished a hot-fudge sundae. Her mother stopped by with a new sweater and her best friend phoned several times to see how she was doing.

After a week or so, everyone resumed their regular routines. Nick remembered now and then to ask LeAnn how she was doing and her professor *did* allow her to retake the exam, but for the most part, life was back to normal. LeAnn's efforts at having a healthier life-style paid off: her color improved, she had more energy, and her dizziness disappeared. But her feelings of emptiness remained.

Although she was very good at pretending, especially around the children, for the most part LeAnn felt like an outsider, a stranger. Life used to be challenging and rewarding. Now she merely went through the motions in a robotlike state. The same was true in her dealings with friends. When she was around people, she felt estranged, as if everyone was communicating in code—all privy to some secret vocabulary she didn't understand. When she and Nick went out socially, instead of being animated and outgoing, she'd sit quietly, nodding perfunctorily when anyone spoke. She usually suggested they leave as soon as possible. She couldn't fathom why everyone seemed so happy.

One evening, coming out of a chamber orchestra concert, Nick and LeAnn were greeted by the season's first snowfall. By the time they drove up in front of their house, the entire yard was covered with a soft, feathery blanket, like a fairy-tale forest. The night was so quiet you could almost hear the snowflakes as they touched the ground.

Nick reached for LeAnn's hand. "Look, honey, isn't it beautiful," he exclaimed, spreading his arms out as if to embrace the entire universe.

"I'm cold," said LeAnn. Then she walked inside and shut the door.

SPIRITUAL DISCONNECTION

The greatest shame of all is that in wanting life to be perfect, we miss out on the truly authentic moments of joy. Like LeAnn, we become isolated, frozen, and removed from those around us. Our senses are deadened. We're rarely receptive to a word spoken in kindness, attuned to the majesty of the sky, the beauty of a sunset or snowflakes sparkling all around.

We're too pressured and anxious and goal-oriented to be grateful when our five-year-old child leaves us a lovingly chosen, carefully picked acorn on our dresser. Immersed in the minutiae, we lose touch with our creativity, with nature, art, work, music— all things that bring meaning and purpose to our lives.

Each individual searches for spiritual connection in her own way. The term "spirituality" usually has religious overtones. Here, it refers to anything that inspires, elevates, and deepens our feelings of wonder and awe.

Many of us experience our spirituality through human ties, especially in those rare moments ·of genuine rapport, when something clicks and we feel understood. When we are connected, whether it's to a person or a family or a whole community of people with whom we share common interests and values, we feel a part of humanity. It is as if by holding one person's hand, we are bound to the next person and the next one and the next. Tragically, women who make themselves indispensable become alienated from their own loved ones.

On her fourth birthday, my daughter Zoe begged me to spend the morning visiting her nursery school. The timing couldn't have been worse; I was finishing a new book proposal that I had sworn would be in the mail by the end of the day. "Please, Mommy, please," she pleaded, eyes wide, imploring me to see how much it meant to her. "I'm going to wear a red birthday crown with tinsel!"

"I'm sorry," I said, guilt bubbling up like bile in my throat. "Next year, I promise."

All day I sat glued to the typewriter, racing against the deadline I'd created. At 5:45, the Federal Express truck drove up. Right then, Gary arrived home with the kids. The kitchen was strewn with typewriter paper. I hadn't showered, and I'd forgotten to pick up the cake. The proposal was finished, a hollow victory at that point. My daughter's birthday comes once a year, and I'd missed it.

Time doesn't wait, and we can't recapture the precious lost moments. We squander our energy and lose sight of what really matters. Over years of putting other people first, we forget who we are, what we're made of, and why we're here on earth. Our own purpose, focus, and commitment get diffused and swallowed up because we don't have any boundaries. Having made ourselves the center of other people's lives, we throw away our own.

I interviewed a woman in her late sixties who had flown in from out-of-town to spend the weekend with her daughter. I was impressed by the ease with which the two shared difficult and painful truths. "I like my independence, but sometimes I wish I had someone to be accountable to," began the daughter, a single thirty-six-year-old securities analyst. "The only person I have to be concerned about is me," she said with a sigh.

By contrast, her mother, eighteen years into a second marriage, said: "I've spent the best years of my life running and schlepping, and making sure everyone else's lives run smoothly. Now the house is empty and I walk from room to room looking for something to do. Maybe I'm looking for myself," she remarked quietly, her mouth turned up in a wry smile. "I'm sixty-eight years old and I'm having an identity crisis."

First and finally, we lose connection with ourselves. We haven't the time or peace to tap our deeper recesses, the part of ourselves that feels holy and connected to God. Most people find it difficult to transcend the details of daily life. Some take time for prayer or meditation; others attend religious services or seek out opportunities for retreat and renewal.

The Indispensable Woman is alienated from her own spirituality. Her life is too hurried, too cluttered with noise and distraction to hear her own inner voice. In her attempts to control every detail, every interaction, and every outcome, she rejects any knowledge of God or a higher power and loses her connection to the natural, sacred flow of life.

Women who make themselves indispensable talk about driving themselves crazy and making themselves sick. They talk about losing their grip, their health, their friends, their marriages, their jobs, and their capacity to savor life and grow from its challenges.

In the early stages, these costs come across like idle complaints; indispensability colors our experience, but doesn't prevent us from functioning successfully. Untreated, the addiction to perfection leads to isolation, failure, and profound despair.

Some people, like LeAnn, are fortunate enough to get help, as she eventually did. Others become sicker, and never recover.

What does it take for Indispensable Women to see what they're doing to themselves? Do they have to hit bottom? What are the catalysts, the turning points that make it possible to step out of the spiral and turn their lives around?

SEVEN

LAST STRAWS, CATALYSTS, AND TURNING POINTS

It usually takes a crisis, sometimes even a devastating event, to recognize how we are hurting ourselves. Knowing the potential costs just isn't enough to motivate most people to change.

We pretend we are fine, or if we aren't fine it doesn't mean anything, or even if it means something surely it will pass. But it doesn't pass. Over time, the physical and emotional exhaustion build and we become inured. We can't remember what feeling good is like, and we go on that way until something happens to shake us out of our complacency.

Women on the other side, who are at some point in recovery, point to an exact moment when denial begins to crack; something occurs that is so threatening, they can no longer ignore the costs of their indispensability. Illness, a setback at work, or the dissolution of a love relationship or a marriage can be the impetus to serious self-examination.

There are three factors inherent in the process of emerging

from denial: A DECREASE IN REWARDS; AN INCREASE IN COSTS; and CONSISTENT NEGATIVE FEEDBACK. Each of these factors occurs simultaneously, building to a crescendo where the need to take action is abundantly clear.

A decrease in rewards

Over time, perfectionism reaches a stage of diminishing returns. What seemed to "work" before, doesn't work as well or at all. Behavior that previously brought comfort, or at least made it possible to function, has less and less of an effect.

An increase in costs

As indispensability's effectiveness wanes, the negative repercussions mount up. The consequences begin to outweigh the rewards. Stress-related health problems become increasingly critical, and coping mechanisms hit an all-time low. Isolation intensifies, and it becomes harder and harder to shake off the sensation that something is seriously wrong.

Consistent negative feedback

The awareness that something is wrong is reinforced by external messages. Concerned friends, co-workers, and family members see you are in trouble, and say so. As they notice and comment on the obvious decline in health, or productivity, or ability to manage your life, their voices echo what you've begun to suspect.

Janis, a free-lance graphic artist, recalls how her need to prove herself and live up to her potential inspired numerous confrontations with friends worried sick at the way she was pushing herself.

"It was about eighteen months since my business had really taken off," she explained. "After years of trying to establish myself, work was finally falling in the door and I wasn't about to turn any of it away." In order to keep up, Janis worked until four A.M.

most nights or until she couldn't keep her eyes open, whichever came first. She'd grab a few hours' sleep and be at it again.

Initially, Janis's friends were glad for her success. But after several months, when it grew apparent her crazy schedule wasn't slowing down, they became openly alarmed. Several people approached her expressing fear she was overdoing it. One evening her best friend arrived unannounced with take-out Chinese food that she insisted Janis sit down and eat. She proceeded to deliver a sermon on the perils of not taking care of yourself, reiterating several times that she loved and supported Janis and didn't want to see her make herself sick. A few of her clients even commented that she seemed worn out; one suggested she take some time off and told her she had given work to another studio because she could see Janis had her hands full.

Denial is very strong. Even when the people we trust most give us clear messages of concern, we do what we can to convince them *and* ourselves that everything is fine. At one point a number of years ago my own weight dropped to ninety-two pounds. Between running myself ragged and trying to have a "perfect" body with no excess fat, I was barely eating.

For a while, virtually everywhere I went someone would comment on how thin I was. Not to be intimidated, I was always prepared with a glib retort, "This is my fighting weight," or, "You can't be too thin or too rich!" I'd say, hoping to divert them from the subject.

What finally got me was the feedback of a complete stranger. I was sitting in our neighborhood restaurant, the Lincoln Del, reading, drinking coffee, and minding my own business, when a chocolate malt appeared out of the blue.

"I didn't order this," I told the waitress.

"Drink up. You need it," she replied.

I went home and took a good, hard look at myself in the mirror, which prompted a good, hard look at my life.

THE STRAW THAT
BROKE THE
CAMEL'S BACK

▼

A particular incident or event usually stands out when women recall what motivated them to change. In my case, the chocolate malt I hadn't ordered was the last straw—the final message that it was time to look at how I was hurting myself and confront my perfectionism.

Last straws present themselves in surprising ways. "I had saved for a year for this keepsake art calendar, which I bought myself for Christmas, not on sale in May, which is when I usually get calendars," recalls Roberta, mother of an emotionally disturbed nineteen-year-old. "When I discovered Sandy had scribbled all over it in purple crayon, I about lost it. Here was the thing I'd wanted for ages, something I'd planned to treasure, and it was ruined."

Another woman talks about finding the Slo-Poke sucker stuck between the handles of her favorite pair of sewing scissors right as she's about to finish hemming the new suit for the luncheon that afternoon. Right then, she knows she's reached the end of her rope. For another, it's the hundredth time her husband fails to take out the garbage before company arrives, or her children demand something without a "please" or "thank you." Another experiences blind fury trying to control a classroom of hostile and sarcastic ninth graders. Still another, a clothing buyer for a classy boutique, goes away on a long weekend to a cabin in the woods. As soon as she's donned her jeans and sweatshirt, she sits down next to a tree and begins to sob.

Teddy, a normally decorous forty-five-year-old executive secretary, can't understand what precipitated her throwing a full-blown temper tantrum at the office.

"I had a lot to do that day, but then I always have a lot to do," she explained. "There was the usual mountain of paperwork on my desk and three lines on hold when my boss stuck a letter under my nose and said he needed it in five minutes. I said, 'You're kidding, right?' He said, 'Time's a-wasting.' I stood up, smacked the desk so hard all the papers went flying and my coffee spilled all over his letter. Then I told him he could type the goddamn thing himself and I walked out!"

Teddy was too emotionally involved to put what happened in perspective. She was convinced the entire incident was caused by her boss's gruffly worded and poorly timed request. But it just happened to come on top of a number of overwhelming and seemingly "unsolvable" pressures.

For almost twelve years, Teddy had been smoldering from her boss's insensitive comments; she was overworked, poorly paid, and grossly underappreciated. Teddy's mother had recently been hospitalized for Alzheimer's disease and she was dashing out each day on her lunch hour and after work to be with her, even on those days her brother or sister were already there. The night preceding the outburst, a distant cousin had arrived on Teddy's doorstep for a week-long surprise visit. She had planned on a quiet, restful weekend; now she felt invaded and pressured to entertain.

It's a mistake to think that the desecrated calendar, the mouthy kid, the too-short deadline, or the unexpected visitor is an isolated incident. The last straws people refer to are almost always part of an ongoing pattern. Maybe you've been doing the lion's share at work for longer than you care to remember. Perhaps you have a long-established habit of putting up with rude behavior or having an "open door" policy, even though friends and family are too thoughtless to think of calling ahead. This time may be one time too many, and you find yourself disproportionately upset to make up for all the times you kept silent in the past. Teddy's "last straw" was the result of unreleased anger accumulated over a long period of time. The incident at work was an accident waiting to happen. Anything could have set it off.

Last straws are merely the tip of the iceberg; provocative episodes that alert us to more serious long-term problems lying beneath the surface. It's common to confuse the last straw with deeper issues. Without further investigation, we can easily dismiss one bad fight or fit of temper as a temporary aberration. Doing so is like bandaging a wound without treating the infection growing underneath.

CATALYSTS

Although it seems as if one minute everything's fine and then suddenly life is a mess, it doesn't really happen that way. A series of events naturally leads to "hitting bottom." These events are catalysts: profound experiences that trigger a dramatic shift in perception.

Catalysts are more far-reaching than last straws. We may go into a tailspin over broken shoelaces and burned dinners, but their impact is short-lived. The kinds of experiences that motivate soul-searching and life-changing decisions are of a more serious nature. When women note the catalysts that cause them to confront their indispensability, they mention serious illness, career changes, family emergencies, financial trauma, relationship transitions, and other significant life crises. There are instances in which a single catalyst causes change; more typically, a number of events converge.

A thirty-six-year-old woman with a master's in social work and a passionate commitment to women's issues fulfills a lifelong dream by becoming director of a rape and sexual assault center. It is a labor of love. She puts in sixty, sometimes seventy hours a week, and though her staff has been carefully chosen, she has the final word on all "important" decisions. She is determined the center operate as a real collective; no male hierarchy here, so she institutes an equal pay-scale for everyone. The secretary earns exactly the same salary that she does, but works half the hours.

Because she cares so much, the woman spends every waking hour counseling, raising money, and working to make the center a success. She never takes time off or leaves for lunch; she can't understand why the others aren't as dedicated. She tries to curb her criticism but they sense it and discuss their grievances behind her back.

One day, she is the only one who comes to work. The others have splintered off and created a new agency, in direct competition. Burned-out and feeling like a failure, she takes a year off to come to terms with what happened. Looking back, she says, "I wanted the right things but I made one very serious mistake. I forgot the difference between being a hero and being a leader."

A painful and protracted divorce is the catalyst in another woman's life. Ilene was initially attracted to the unique blend of outdoorsman and artist she saw in Will. A Vietnam vet and ex-hippie, Will had simple aspirations: a cabin in the woods and the freedom to write. Ilene, who had been raised by terribly ambitious parents, was touched by the simplicity of Will's dreams. She vowed to encourage and support his writing.

Ilene *hadn't* bargained for having to provide full support for herself, Will, and their twin sons, once they were born. A writer of considerable talent, Will was only occasionally able to find paying work. Most of the time he started stories, but became bored or depressed and wasn't able to finish. Drafts for two half-written novels and scores of story outlines sat in piles in his office. Ilene's career in management meant long hours and a forty-five-minute commute to the city. She'd pick up the kids at day-care on the way home, make dinner, and then fall into bed around ten, at which point Will usually disappeared into his study. They barely saw each other, and when they did, Will was either sullen or scorned her for caring about material success. They became increasingly estranged.

Had they been able to communicate, there might have been hope. But Will became more and more withdrawn and unwilling to deal with their problems. "I would have moved mountains to make it work," said Ilene. "Talking to him was like pulling teeth. He wouldn't say anything of consequence for days, and then, a little show of interest and I'd pounce as if he'd made the most loving and meaningful gesture." Ilene made excuses to their friends, their parents, their sons. It took fifteen years for her to finally leave. Even then, she wasn't sure she had done the right thing.

For a third woman, learning she had breast cancer shocked her into reevaluating the lack of support in her life. In her words, "For the first time, I really understood that my time on earth is limited. I faced the possibility that I might not be here tomorrow, in which case my family, who had always depended on me so much, would have to take care of themselves. Knowing that has made it easier for me to stop making myself indispensable."

For these three women, it took wrenching experiences for them to examine their indispensability and reevaluate the quality of their lives. In each of their cases, traumas served as catalysts. However, catalysts can spring from favorable circumstances as well.

A new job, a new baby, or moving to a different home or city can be a catalyst. Adjusting to dramatic change, even when it's an occasion for optimism and celebration, can jolt us out of existing patterns of behavior. Whether stimulated by positive or negative events, catalysts serve an important purpose: they disturb the status quo and spark the need for change.

HITTING BOTTOM: A NEW BEGINNING

When someone says they've "hit bottom," they usually mean they've reached the lowest imaginable point: a point where a number of catalysts have maneuvered inner shifts in perception and a last straw has tipped the scales, prompting a pivotal, powerful, inescapable moment of truth.

The term "hitting bottom" conveys pain, disappointment, and despair. It implies failure. Yet it's exactly these experiences that, almost without exception, provide positive opportunities for personal growth.

Crises can be important turning points. The lost job, family emergency, or falling out with a dear friend can be the perfect opening for creating a new, healthier way of being. But first there is always an ending. Not all endings are concrete. A loss of trust or a change in deeply held beliefs can also be an ending, and one of grave consequence.

In *Transitions: Making Sense of Life's Changes,* author William Bridges contends that all transitions begin with an ending. He cites four different aspects that are part of every ending: DISENGAGEMENT (a breakdown or separation from the existing system), DISIDENTIFICATION (loss of past ways of identifying oneself), DISENCHANTMENT (change in the perception of reality), and DISORIENTATION (losing one's bearings).[1]

Bridges's model is useful in exploring the process of hitting bottom experienced by the Indispensable Woman. For example, consider Claire, the rape-center director discussed earlier whose burning commitment to her career resulted in her one-woman show becoming a one-woman agency.

The first stage Claire entered when she hit bottom was disengagement. She physically separated herself from work and changed her familiar surroundings. Next, Claire experienced disidentification. Her identity shifted from being head of a progressive women's center to thinking of herself as screwed-up and out of a job. Third, Claire lost her hope and her idealism. She became disenchanted with the dream of rescuing rape victims and her belief in the feasibility of a women's center free of traditional power struggles and politicking. Finally, in hitting bottom, she became disoriented. During her two years as executive director, she had navigated with a firm sense of purpose and direction. Now she felt frighteningly lost and alone.

In the midst of her crisis, Claire would have said her life was falling apart. And on one level, that was true. However, her year that began in turmoil turned out to be valuable and rich.

During her hiatus, Claire had time to sort out her value system; many of her beliefs and philosophies had been formed in her mid-twenties and needed tempering. She had the chance to rethink her politics and found that, while she was still dedicated to serving women, she would be better off working in an already established agency, without the added responsibilities of fundraising and outreach. Claire was able to attain some distance and perspective. Most important, she drew closer to herself and found solace in reading, long walks, and solitude; she made a commitment to integrate time for herself into her life-style.

TURNING POINTS

It's common for people to look back on the most painful periods of their lives and realize with amazement that they were positive *turning points*. Having hit bottom, we see life through new eyes. Attitudes are altered, major change results, or we may gain a deeper acceptance and appreciation of the significance of exactly where we are.

Thinking of hitting bottom as a positive turn of events is a little like thanking your lucky stars when you wake up with the flu. In fact, some medical schools of thought contend that certain illnesses are the body's way of releasing toxins and cleansing itself; getting sick can be a positive and natural sign that the body needs different or better care.

On the surface, the "Dear Jane" letter or close-call car accident isn't cause for celebration. But taken in a larger context, the seemingly unfortunate twist ends up just the opposite.

Typically, turning points happen when misfortune intersects with hope. According to Rhoda F. Levin, a therapist who specializes in coping with life passages, people may change for a couple of reasons: they either get kicked so long and so hard they can't stand it anymore, or they are inspired to change in order to have a deeper, more satisfying life. Levin says, "Most often, both of these forces operate simultaneously. Something difficult or painful occurs so that the individual becomes increasingly vulnerable. At the same time, there is a growing yearning for connection, for personal transformation, for peace. In this intricate dance of push/pull, the person inches slowly toward the most challenging of all human endeavors—change."

VITAL
WARNING SIGNS

Is it necessary to hit bottom in order to break the pattern of indispensability? Or is it possible to intervene and act before it reaches crisis proportions?

There's a wonderfully simple poem that depicts the oh-so-human tendency to repeat the mistakes many times before finally "getting it."

POEM IN FIVE CHAPTERS
Portia Nelson

I

I walk down the street
There is a deep hole in the sidewalk.
I fall in.
I am lost—I am helpless
        It isn't my fault
It takes forever to find a way out.

II

I walk down the same street
There is a deep hole in the sidewalk
I pretend I don't see it
I fall in again.
I can't believe I am in the same place but it
      isn't my fault
It still takes a long time to get out.

III

I walk down the same street
There is a deep hole in the sidewalk.
I see it is there
I still fall in . . . It's a habit
My eyes are open
I know where I am
It is my fault
I get out immediately.

IV

I walk down the same street
There is a deep hole in the sidewalk
I walk around it.

V

I walk down another street.[2]

The holes are there, to be sure. We stumble, we fall, we pull
ourselves out again. It is hoped that we can learn the lessons before
causing ourselves more pain than need be. Still, I've seen women
whose denial is so forceful, they suffer enormous consequences
without seeing that change is in order.

Whether a person hits bottom or becomes sufficiently aware
of the costs of indispensability to head off the most severe consequences, in either case, there is always a turning point. The turning point is that moment of naked acceptance of the truth. Denial
falls away like scales from our eyes. Rationalizations suddenly
look like poor excuses to keep ourselves stuck.

Once we recognize the truth, before real change is possible,
we must acknowledge that perfectionism has taken over our lives,
that it is out of our control.

Accepting powerlessness is unquestionably one of the most
difficult of all paradoxes to grasp; it is anathema to the Indispensable Woman in her need to believe she is in control. Yet it is only
when we can admit that in our compulsion to overachieve and
make everything run perfectly, we are running ourselves into the
ground—only then will we begin to consider the alternatives. Only

when we accept that the very foundation on which we are building our relationships is shaky and full of holes, only when we realize that what we thought was giving our life meaning is actually draining us dry, only when we see that we are hurting ourselves and that we don't know how to stop, is there a real chance of turning our lives around.

Each woman's process of coming to terms with the truth is unique to her own background and particular set of circumstances. The process doesn't have to culminate in causing irreparable damage.

These warning signals will help you identify the "holes" before hitting bottom. No one symptom alone is cause for concern. Danger is indicated if you consistently experience a number of the following:

PHYSICAL SIGNS

Exhaustion

Insomnia

Excessive need for sleep

Significant change in appetite

Chronic colds and sore throats

Back problems

Headaches

Frequent indigestion, nausea, or diarrhea

Lethargy

Hyperventilation

Blurred vision

Accelerated pulse rate

Hypertension

Facial tics

Shortness of breath

Hair loss

Noticeable changes in sexual drive

Skin disorders

Significant weight loss or gain

MENTAL SIGNS

Trouble concentrating

Forgetfulness

Disorientation

Reduced productivity

Making mistakes

Covering up mistakes

Shortened attention span

Inability to prioritize and problem-solve

Difficulties listening when other people speak

Lack of perspective

Circular thinking

BEHAVIORAL SIGNS

General apathy

Leaving projects half-finished

Becoming antisocial and cut off from friends

Impatience

Lashing out and irrational blaming

Being highly critical and intolerant

Seeing things in black and white terms

Increased arguing and conflicts with friends or family

Loss of interest in hobbies

Feeling rushed

Eating on the run

Increased use of alcohol and drugs

Chronic lateness

Decline in exercise and other physical release

Binge/purge cycles of activity, such as frantic errand-running followed by staring in a stupor at the TV

EMOTIONAL SIGNS

Feeling isolated, cut off

Defensiveness

Obsessive worrying

Mood swings

Crying jags

Feeling victimized, unappreciated, or misunderstood

Loss of sense of humor

Boredom

Free-floating anxiety

Frequent anger and resentment

Rising feelings of hostility or rage

Powerlessness

Detachment

Depression

Despair

Suicide fantasies

SPIRITUAL SIGNS

No sense of purpose

Alienation/estrangement

Reluctance to make commitments

Disillusionment

Cynicism

Inability to appreciate nature, music, and art

Loss of faith in a higher power

Inability to get in touch with feelings of gratefulness and joy

Lack of capacity to express and accept love

Feelings of emptiness

Whether we see the abyss from a safe distance, perch precariously on the brink, or fall all the way in, getting scared only takes us so far. A glimpse of disaster creates an intensified commitment to take better care of ourselves in order to hold on to what we have. However, permanent change requires two things: the willingness to face current reality *and* the ability to envision an alternative way of life.

People respond to a personal crisis or turning point by altering behavior, life-style, or relationships, but often the change is short-lived. Having an immediate scare *does* motivate reassessment and change. The last-chance performance review, serious altercation, or borderline X ray is usually enough to shake a person up. A survivor of cardiac bypass surgery quits smoking, starts exercising, and follows a healthful diet, grateful for a second chance at life. A woman whose perfectionism lands her in the hospital with exhaustion, or all alone wondering what went wrong in her relationships, is apt to reevaluate her basic beliefs and may even be willing to relax her expectations, at least for a while.

As the crisis or turning point fades further into the distance, however, most individuals become less motivated and start to veer from the "program." Commitment wanes for three reasons: The emotional impact of the crisis wears off; change only occurs on a superficial level; or the individual isn't able to envision the potential rewards. Any one or combination of these factors may inhibit long-term change. The same arrogance that protects us from believing anything bad could happen to us conveniently dulls our memories once the immediate scare passes. As soon as life is back to "normal," we forget how sick or terrified or threatened we felt, and with that, we relapse into our old and comfortable ways.

Even when scare tactics result in major change, there may not be an inner transformation. For example, the recovering cardiac patient may cut back on salt or watch her weight, but unless she embraces the overall connections between diet, exercise, lifestyle, and health, her chances of long-term success are fairly slim. In the same way, the Indispensable Woman, acknowledging there is too much pressure in her life, might delegate or abdicate some of her responsibility. Still, unless she comes to understand and accept how her perfectionism and stress fit together, she'll soon reclaim the responsibilities or find new ones to replace them.

Sustaining real change is only possible when we can consistently imagine the rewards on the other side. The threat of loss might set the wheels in motion, but a belief in what there is to gain is needed to carve out a new path and *stay on it*. We must be able to grasp the concrete advantages and directly experience or anticipate rewards to stay focused and committed. Otherwise, resolutions are held in place by fear or threat or pride or "white knuckling,"³ and can only endure for so long.

TOWARD A
POSITIVE VISION
▼

Throughout this book we have seen the origins, rewards, and risks of perfectionism. We have seen how we become addicted to indispensability and the intense degree of denial that keeps us from acknowledging the need to change.

Even when we hit bottom, it is terrifying to consider giving up indispensability because we are bereft of an alternative vision. We have no concept of what it might be like *not* to make ourselves indispensable.

But let your imagination flow for a moment. What *would* it be like to stop carrying the weight of the world on your shoulders? What benefits might accompany giving up the goal of perfectionism? How would your days be filled? How would you feel? Is there an alternative to making yourself indispensable?

Yes, there is. The alternative to making yourself indispensable is allowing yourself to be human. Humanness doesn't require perfection; it acknowledges needs, accepts limitations, and only asks that you give your best.

The vast rewards of giving up the perfection addiction are present in every area of life. By acknowledging needs, the possibility of support comes into view. Consider the time and energy freed up in taking responsibility for only *your* share. Imagine the relief of not assuming every outcome rests solely on your direct input.

Greater satisfaction can be found at work and in other involvements when you are able to accept limitations and know your best effort is enough. When you stop pushing yourself to achieve beyond what is reasonable and comfortable, you gain a heightened regard for what is accomplished. Since everything doesn't have to be perfect, you can appreciate the actual gains that are made. In turn, your self-esteem improves from experiencing success, which before was out of reach.

There is the opportunity for real growth in personal relationships. Indispensability destroys any hope of equality. Only by accepting a more human image of yourself is there potential for equal give-and-take. Setting yourself up as a perfect mate, friend, mother, or lover actually erects a barrier preventing the flow of communication, trust, and love. By encouraging your loved ones' dependency you limit them and miss out on the pleasure of letting yourself be nurtured and taken care of.

Giving up the mantle of perfectionism has the potential to bring serenity and peace. There is relief in relinquishing control and knowing there are powers at work beyond your own. It is immensely comforting to accept being part of a greater plan of which you are neither author nor overseer. When you stop playing God, you may discover new or renewed faith.

CHANGE BEGINS WITH OURSELVES

It takes great courage and tenacity to confront an addictive pattern of behavior. Women who engage in the process of giving up their indispensability know there is a lot to gain as well as a lot to lose. When we step out of set roles we upset an intricate balance, which often makes those involved uncomfortable, fearful, and angry. They feel defensive, interpreting our change as a personal challenge. They may resist the new order, which they may feel is anything from irritating to unfair to outrageous, because it calls upon them to alter their own behavior.

There is no question that recovery from indispensability threatens the smooth functioning of relationships. Particularly in situations where division of labor is gender-linked and financial security means toeing the line, the potential retaliation is real and frightening. Many women perceive that altering their public images as superwomen may provoke marital strife and jeopardize career gains, a fear that is also well-grounded in reality.

Having created an expectation of indispensability and sold it to our employers, mates, parents, children, and friends, naturally we can expect them to grumble, moan, and, in some cases, kick, scream, and threaten to call in a replacement if we don't deliver the goods. Practically speaking, we've backed ourselves into a corner.

The way out is to ask for what you need. The biggest reason women give for why they have to keep doing everything themselves is that there is simply no one else to do it. "Have you asked?" is always my first question. "What's the point?" is almost always the answer—this from women who congratulate themselves on assertiveness!

The truth is, there's no way to know without trying. We can assume our children can't wait, our employers can't be flexible, our husbands can't help, our lovers can't be intimate, our friends can't be there for us the way we want them to be, but unless we're willing to come forward and ask for what we need, it's all speculation. We complain and moan and carry on till the cows come home, but as long as we keep doing it ourselves, nothing will change. Passively staying indispensable is actually an active choice to keep things the way they are.

And what about the woman who does speak up and pays for it by losing her job, or her friends, or a mate who leaves her in search of another, preferably indispensable, woman? There are no guarantees that recovery won't provoke the need for changing circumstances or severing personal relationships. Transitions are difficult, but painful choices are a necessary part of human growth.

Ideally, the significant people in your life will be receptive and supportive of your desire to grow. It is hoped that they will demonstrate their support by not standing in your way. Perhaps they will examine their own behavior and change with you. Perhaps not.

We can ask, we can encourage, we can express our gratitude and appreciation when others take positive steps. But ultimately, we cannot change other people. Through a serious and whole-hearted commitment to recovery, we *can* change ourselves.

EIGHT

FINDING YOUR BALANCE

More than half the battle of making any serious life change is identifying the problem and deciding to do something about it. Having recognized how your perfectionism is affecting your life, it's a relief to know there's a way to tackle and overcome it. Now comes the "take action" part—the time to take positive, concrete steps toward stopping your drive to be indispensable.

Depending on how you look at it, recovery can be a difficult, painstaking task, or a fun and challenging opportunity. In fact, it is a little of each. It is hard work *and* the rewards are immediate and plentiful.

The process of recovery is qualitatively different from having a problem, addressing it, and moving on. There are no simple rules, magic formulas, or quick-fix solutions for beating the perfection addiction. There *are* guidelines that, if followed, provide a road map of long-term change. The goal is a happier, healthier, more balanced existence. The process involves giving up trying to control everything around you and adopting more human expectations.

Most people associate "recovery" with illness. You get sick —you recover. But the concept has a broader definition, extending beyond the scope of physical illness. Whether an individual is recovering from alcoholism, an eating disorder, overspending, or perfectionism, progress is a daily pursuit.

Maybe your perfectionism isn't full-blown or manifests itself primarily in one area of your life. Having had the benefit of recognizing your perfectionism through the many different stories shared in this book, take the opportunity to do something *now*, at whatever point you happen to be in your life. The risks only increase, and the more ingrained the patterns of indispensability become, the more difficult they are to break. There's no conceivable reason for putting off change.

TEN STEPS TOWARD LIVING HAPPILY WITH IMPERFECTION

Most recovery programs have been modeled, to a greater or lesser degree, after the Twelve Step tradition of Alcoholics Anonymous.[1] The steps governing recovery from perfectionism are based on similar principles.

1. See your life as it is

2. Accept personal responsibility

3. Examine your assumptions

4. Give yourself permission to acknowledge your feelings

5. Identify your needs

6. Simplify

7. Seek support

8. Let go of guilt

9. Learn to see the humor

10. Create real and reachable goals

While these steps are arranged so one flows naturally to the next, it is also perfectly fine to move around from one step to another. No single step has greater significance or gravity; what matters most is considering each in a way that maximizes its impact. Every person's recovery follows its own path.

Recovery doesn't take place outside of and separate from day-to-day life. There's no way to "stop the world and get off" so you can concentrate solely on ridding yourself of indispensability. The opposite is true: Your life *is* the natural practice ground for learning new ways of ineracting, handling stress, and coping with responsibility. Although most people describe important life changes as if they happened suddenly, even embellishing the dramatic moments, enduring change rarely is the product of a startling epiphany. Real change—that filters down through all parts of your life—is more likely to come as a result of ordinary, everyday, small yet significant progress.

As you work through each step you will reach a point where you comprehend its implications and begin to incorporate your understanding of it into your life. However, since recovery is fluid, there is no such thing as ever *completing* a step. Rather, your grasp of and relationship to each part continually grows and deepens over time.

No one rushes into making important life changes as if they were waiting with bated breath for someone to hand them an invitation. It's natural to experience fear, sadness, and anger when contemplating giving up addictive behavior—anger at having to relinquish the rewards that came with indispensability; sadness, even grief at losing a part of yourself that's familiar and feels secure; and fear of what lies on the other side.

Women in recovery speak glowingly of enduring rewards and

make a concentrated effort at sustaining them. Ultimately, making a commitment takes a leap of faith and a lot of encouragement. Some measure of ambivalence signifies respect for the seriousness of the endeavor.

HEALING
THE WHOLE PERSON
▼

When dealing with difficult challenges we all tend to play from our strengths. One woman describes herself as "the intellectual type"; she copes by logically thinking things through. Another is terribly practical, a "doer" whose response is to snap into action. Still another turns first and foremost to spiritual resources. Overcoming the perfection addiction requires a holistic approach to change. The mind, body, and spirit are intricately related and must all be involved. The whole person must heal, not just in one area, but by galvanizing all available resources.

While it's natural to lead with the part of yourself you feel most confident about, the most successful recovery calls upon all facets in working toward change. It isn't enough to utilize strictly mental tools through prioritizing, problem solving, or rethinking your assumptions and expectations. And coming at the problem from an exclusively emotional plane won't necessarily solve practicalities. Feeling connected to a higher power is important, too, but not enough, in and of itself, to sustain change.

If we are truly to recover, transformation must take place in all areas of our lives. We cannot concentrate on improving our health and then turn around and ignore the problems in our relationships. Or focus on spiritual growth, but keep making ourselves indispensable at the office. Or get smart about saying no to other people, without remembering to say yes to ourselves. For these reasons, the ten steps have been developed with an emphasis on integrating mental, emotional, and spiritual tools.

THE STEPS

Within each step there is a discussion of what the step means, why it's important, and how it's best approached. In addition, roadblocks are identified, followed by practical suggestions for overcoming them.

STEP ONE: SEE YOUR LIFE AS IT IS

Seeing your life as it is *means* you quit pretending everything is just fine. It means you stop rationalizing and believing that if you are only perfect enough, you will be able to put all the pieces together. It means achieving perspective—pulling back and putting your life into a larger context.

Seeing yourself as valuable, rather than essential, as part of the universe—not the center of the universe—is the first step toward recovery from perfectionism. At present, you're convinced you really *are* indispensable. Your vantage point puts you in the most pivotal position; you genuinely believe everything revolves around your assistance, involvement, and support. Yet on the rare occasion when you just can't be available, because of sickness, or timing, or other conflicts, the world doesn't fall apart.

Even if you know that intellectually, it's still hard to take an objective view of your own life. You keep putting on blinders and repeating the same behavior. When you honestly face that your perfectionism and drive to be indispensable are harming you and the people around you, constructive steps can be taken to change that behavior.

How do you begin to see your life as it is? Through HONEST EXAMINATION and PERSPECTIVE.

The *importance* of honest examination is that it gives you realistic and updated information on how you're really doing. Start by going back to basics:

Stop:

You needn't give notice at work or extricate yourself from your primary relationship; just interrupt your daily schedule and make some time to think about your life. Try to cease the immersion in activity, the internal racing around, and simply be still instead.

Look:

Next, you need to face facts. Perfectionism is a vicious cycle in which your self-esteem is based on attaining an impossible goal. The painful truth is, you aren't perfect, you'll never be perfect, and trying isn't getting you anywhere good.

Taking a personal inventory is one way to get a handle on reality. Start by listing each separate aspect of your life. For example, your list might include: Health, Work, Relationship with Mate, Friendships, Leisure Time, and Exercise. Next, evaluate each aspect on the basis of EFFECTIVENESS (how well you are managing) and PERSONAL SATISFACTION (your level of contentment and happiness).

Taking a personal inventory is hard, but fight the temptation to rationalize or run away from looking closely at yourself. If you realize you're consistently tired and run-down, take this seriously as a sign that stress may be wearing down your resistance. Or if you see that you have been so busy, important friendships are going by the wayside, your marriage is suffering, or your time for yourself is at such a premium three minutes alone in the bathroom is a luxury, consider this valuable information. Notice what shape your life is in, without making excuses or glossing over any part of it.

Listen:

Listening includes taking in other people's input, along with hearing your own voice. It's what helps you correctly interpret the data you collect and understand its meaning.

External feedback is an invaluable aid in seeing how you are hurting yourself. Especially when worded in a loving and sensitive way, it provides essential, objective information. It's natural to feel defensive in the face of other people's comments. Try to push through any feelings of shame or embarrassment.

It's just as important to listen to your own inner voice—the one that tells you how tired and drained and sick to death you are of taking care of everyone else's needs. This may be the angry, resentful voice, complaining about too many demands and not enough support. It may be the nagging one, reminding you it's been six months since you took so much as a day off, let alone a real vacation. Or the sad and wistful one, expressing regret that in the process of making yourself indispensable, life seems to be passing you by. Or the challenging voice that inquires, "Don't you deserve better?"

Along with being attuned to your inner voice, try to become aware of your speaking voice. Recognizing what and how you communicate—the messages you convey—is an essential part of an honest examination of your life. It's common to not really hear yourself. When you do, you may be surprised, even shocked, by how you sound.

After tracking herself for an entire week, Robin, an airline stewardess and mother of a three-year-old, was taken aback by how she sounded. She says, "I've always thought of myself as soft-spoken and unassuming. But that's the opposite of how I come across. I spent half the time complaining about how much I had to do, and the rest of the time, I was terse and defensive, especially when I was trying to get my son to behave, or my husband to help me." Another woman, Mary-Ann, discovered her voice usually sounded either urgent or impatient. She found that several times a day she made the statement, sometimes to another person, sometimes into thin air, "I can't believe how much I have to do. I'll never get it all done!"

The tone we assume and the messages we communicate say a lot about our lives. We don't mean to sound anxious or demanding or controlling; our voices betray the stress we are experiencing. Listening carefully to external feedback, to our inner voice, and to how we relate tells us a lot about how we are doing. Listening requires we let down both the barriers we've set up to keep other people at a distance and those we've erected to protect ourselves from the truth.

When you're caught up in the throes of obsessive behavior, you can't see what you're doing to yourself and those around you. Your perception is skewed; it's as if you're going round and round in endless circles with no way out. With perspective, you picture yourself from different and more expansive frames of reference. In doing so, you realize you are not alone and that help is possible, and you gain hope, essential in order to make positive strides in your life.

Altering your normal routines is one way to gain perspective. You might modify your schedule, temporarily withdraw from a few of your regular responsibilities, or decline to take on any new ones. For instance, if your usual morning routine is to jump out of bed, grab a quick cup of coffee, get dressed, and rush off to work, try setting your alarm for a half hour earlier and use that time to read the paper and enjoy a leisurely, nourishing breakfast. Or you might "resign" from handling a particular responsibility, and use that time to relax and reflect. Given your present pace, making one small change or opening up a free, unscheduled hour in the week could affect your entire attitude and point of view.

Another way to get perspective is through connection to something that draws you outside and beyond yourself. When you are absorbed in details and constant demands, it's easy to lose touch with the big picture. If you can allow yourself to be open and receptive, there's nothing like a long walk or the resonance of beautiful music to bring your life back into focus. Or make a point of spending time with a special friend you rarely see, especially one whose life is different from your own, who might be able to offer a new outlook. Involvement in something new and apart from the norm—perhaps pursuing an interest you've long had but were too busy to develop, or an activity that, for you, is out of character, like roller-skating or piano lessons, is another way to extricate yourself from the circular maze of indispensability.

Perspective also comes from being attuned to a greater purpose in your life. For many people, spirituality is the bridge between self-absorption in personal concerns—getting lost in the nitty-gritty of day-to-day trivia—and seeing themselves in relation to a broader vision. Getting in touch with spirituality helps people make sense of their lives and put things in place.

The term "spirituality" is often used synonymously with organized religion or belief in God. In fact, it is anything that helps you transcend your daily concerns and connect with the rest of the human race. For one person, that connection comes through participation in family holiday gatherings or attending religious services; for another individual, solitude is most conducive to prayer and meditation. Many people experience their spirituality in relation to others, through fellowship and community. I find, sometimes, that spending just a little bit of concentrated time with my children helps me see the forest for the trees and remember what it's all about.

The great paradox is that we are all, in fact, indispensable. Each and every one of us is a unique human being, an essential player in a greater scheme. Being addicted to perfection, we either denigrate ourselves for not being "enough" or overcompensate by assuming we have too much power. Staying in tune with spirituality—in whatever way is personally meaningful—helps us know there is something greater than ourselves, that we are not responsible for everything, that we are a loved and valued and necessary part of humanity.

ROADBLOCKS

Perfectionism, by its nature, presents an inherent roadblock to seeing your life as it is. The very idea that perfection is attainable impedes your ability to have a clear picture of reality. How can your life possibly be out of control? If there are problems, shouldn't you be smart, enterprising, or motivated enough to come up with a solution?

Recovery asks that you give up your most treasured belief: that through will, effort, and energy you are capable of controlling what happens. It goes totally against the grain to stop trying to control and to submit, in some cases, to letting what happens happen, or even doing nothing at all. (Try being totally involved in a heated argument without having the last word. Try sitting in the same room with dirty dishes for one hour without washing them.) One big reason why we end up doing so much is that we find it virtually impossible to *not do anything*.

Time and space—two crucial elements in gaining perspective—are also major roadblocks for Indispensable Women.

It is virtually impossible to put things in perspective when you're always in the eye of the storm. The obsession with filling up every hour and the fear of setting limits and saying no prevents the quiet time needed for reflection.

PRACTICALLY SPEAKING...

Examining your life involves naming what you see. Labeling a problem is a way of getting a concrete handle on it, so you can begin dealing with it. Some people label by verbalizing the problem to themselves or to another person. For example, you might say: "My obsessive perfectionism is causing serious problems in my life," or, "By making myself indispensable, I am making myself sick." Many people find it useful to write in a journal or notebook. There is something about the printed word that gives added credibility.

As you look honestly at your life, you may choose to seek help. Going for help validates your feelings and clarifies the issues. Some women find it safest and most productive to confront their problems with the help of a professional counselor. Others are most comfortable checking out their feelings with a concerned friend. If you choose to begin therapy at this point, I recommend working with someone who will both help you understand the origins of perfectionism and integrate balance into your life.

People achieve perspective in a great many ways. Here are a variety of recommendations:

Take a good look at yourself in the mirror. (Notice how your appearance reflects your level of stress.)

Talk with other people.

Talk to yourself.

Talk to a therapist.

Be alone.

Be outside.

Be silent.

Attend church or synagogue services; participate in spiritual rituals.

Keep a journal.

Write letters to a friend.

Listen to music.

Sit in the dark.

Read a good book.

Hold a baby.

Volunteer to do charitable work that is satisfying, pleasurable, and helps you get your mind off yourself. (Remember: This isn't a job. You're contributing your time!)

Take long walks and notice the scenery.

Exercise.

Go on a vacation.

Envision looking back at yourself at a ripe old age.

It isn't enough to take up these activities and do them once or twice; getting perspective depends on integrating them into your regular routine. Your perspective won't change unless your priorities change. That means *making* time for what's important. A three-day weekend is terrific, but by Tuesday afternoon you're back on the treadmill. One vigorous aerobics class, one special afternoon spent sharing with a good friend, attending a lecture, or sitting quietly in church gets you inspired, but only makes a difference over the long haul if it becomes a routine and consistent part of your life.

STEP TWO: ACCEPT PERSONAL RESPONSIBILITY

Take *more* responsibility? The operative word is "personal." You're terrific at taking responsibility for everyone and everything in sight. In doing so, you shift your focus outward instead of seeing your own part in making yourself indispensable.

You accept personal responsibility when you quit blaming others for the pressure in your life. When you look at how *you've* set up the patterns of perfectionism and ask what *you* get out of them. When you stop feeling like a victim in impossible circumstances and see that it's up to you to heal the past and embrace the future.

How to take responsibility begins with recognizing that *you* are the source of your pressure rather than attributing it to external causes. Recovery is contingent on acknowledging your complicity in perpetuating the patterns of addiction. Your admirers may cheer you on, encourage, and cajole you to be indispensable, but you and you alone are liable for your actions.

Next, taking personal responsibility involves accepting consequences. Making the connection between your perfectionism and resulting problems in your health, spiritual well-being, career, and relationships is key to recovery. Once you see in what ways your behavior is self-destructive, you're more motivated to make changes.

A third step in taking responsibility requires making amends, first to yourself, then to others you may have hurt. Women in this stage of recovery often are surprised to find their perfectionism has created hardship or injustice. One woman, in retrospect, saw that her indispensability was a way of keeping a tight rein on her husband. She said, "I always stayed right on top of everything, trying to anticipate his needs and making sure he knew what he was supposed to be doing. Fifteen minutes wouldn't go by without my reminding him to call the plumber or asking if he'd gotten tickets for the game or suggesting he'd probably feel better if he took a shower before dinner. I thought I was being caring, but now it's obvious I was choking him. And driving a wedge between us."

With the help of a family therapist, this woman realized her need to control was the only way she knew of getting love. Once she saw how she was hurting her relationship with her husband, she was able to apologize and back off. In turn, he reassured her that his love was based not on being dependent on her for management and mothering, but on his appreciation of her as a person.

Making amends is important because it's a direct, sometimes public form of expressing personal responsibility. Asking forgiveness, of yourself and those you've hurt, settles the score, heals wounds, and releases you from holding on to old pain. Apologizing doesn't mean you're a bad person. It doesn't imply maliciousness, stupidity, or intentional wrongdoing. Saying "I'm sorry" simply means you know your behavior has caused harm and you wish to remedy the situation.

ROADBLOCKS

There are two primary roadblocks to taking personal responsibility: PRIDE and PREOCCUPATION. The Indispensable Woman can't risk facing her fallibility. Even if she did, she hasn't the time to do anything about it.

Seeing your part in making yourself indispensable, and acknowledging the need for change, punctures the illusion of perfection. Perfect people don't make mistakes. They don't have problems. They certainly aren't in need of recovery!

Preoccupation with the details of everyone else's lives is another obstacle to taking responsibility. Indispensability provides the perfect out: How can you be bothered to think about yourself when so many people need and count on you? It's safer to concentrate on others; being consumed in caretaking distracts you from exploring your own issues and focusing on recovery.

Warning: Other people may offer you ways of getting off the hook. It's typical for friends and family to burst in with all sorts of excuses and justifications when you share your newfound sense of responsibility. Beware of responses such as "Oh, you're just trying to be helpful" and "Of course you aim for perfection, and look how close you've come!" These kinds of statements are flattering, but don't help further your recovery.

Another warning: Don't be a perfectionist about taking responsibility for the past. Making amends is for the present. Do what you can and move on.

PRACTICALLY SPEAKING...

There are some concrete tools that support looking at yourself in a new way.

Each time you feel compelled to push yourself or are on the verge of accepting another demand, stop and ask yourself first: "Who's making me do this?" If the answer is "I am," then decide whether it's really necessary for you to take on another duty. If the feelings of pressure are coming from external sources, it's your choice whether or not to take responsibility.

Interrupt your thoughts whenever you catch yourself lamenting how pressured you feel. Ask yourself what can be done about it. Is the pressure real or imagined? Are you exaggerating it? If so, stop yourself.

Visual imagery is another useful tool in replacing one set of images with another. As the Indispensable Woman, you envision yourself burdened by everyone's demands. Instead, imagine yourself on a desert island without a phone or any connection to reality. Then take a temporary side-trip back home and look at how everyone is managing without you. Are you *really* indispensable? In whose eyes?

Affirmations—positive statements that reinforce a new way of thinking—are another practical aid in taking responsibility. Create one or two affirmations and repeat them to yourself often. You might consider:

"I am completely responsible for myself."

"I choose everything I take on."

"I am more than what I do."

"My recovery is in my own hands."

STEP THREE: EXAMINE YOUR ASSUMPTIONS

The third step of recovery stresses the importance of carefully examining your assumptions to see how they're influencing your behavior.

The assumptions you carry with you, and the expectations created out of them, have developed over many, many years. What you think and believe—how you see yourself and the world—may or may not correspond to reality. Your assumptions may be faulty or need to be updated or discarded totally.

There are five categories of assumptions that set up expectations of perfectionism and indispensability: EXAGGERATIONS; ABSOLUTES; ULTIMATUMS; TRUISMS; and EXCUSES. Let's see how each works:

EXAGGERATIONS have some basis in reality, but are distortions. Examples are
"I'm the only one who can do it."
"Everyone is depending on me."

ABSOLUTES are the unequivocal rules we set for our own behavior. They are usually role-related, such as

"Perfect employees never make mistakes."

"Good mothers are always available to their children."

ULTIMATUMS warn of impending danger. They are phrased as either/or statements, such as

"If I don't hold it together, it will all fall apart."

"I better be perfect, or they'll find out I'm no good."

TRUISMS refer to beliefs we've adopted, whether or not they're really *true*. They come from a hodgepodge of sources, including famous quotes, family folklore, and superstition. Well-known truisms include:

"The more you do, the more you're worth."

"Practice makes perfect."

EXCUSES are the assumptions we fall back on to rationalize our behavior. We keep ourselves stuck by repeating the following sentences:

"It's easier to do it myself."

"Sooner or later there'll be time for me."

Each of these assumptions can be altered, updated, or traded for one that is more realistic. For instance:

"I'm the only one who can do it."

Is there *anyone* else who could *possibly* do it? It might be more correct to say something like "I'm the most willing, best prepared, or most available one to do it," which makes the idea of not doing it a little easier to consider.

"Perfect employees never make mistakes."

This assumption contains two glaring misconceptions. To begin with, there's no such thing as a perfect employee. Second, no one is above making a mistake. You might replace this assumption with a more realistic statement like "Committed employees try to do their best." That gives you room to be human.

"If I don't hold it together, it will all fall apart."

This assumption is false; your absence may cause aggravation but it probably won't be catastrophic. And the vagueness makes it difficult to know just what the "it" is that is about to fall apart. A more appropriate statement might be: "If I'm not able or willing to take on a certain responsibility, this may result in problems or the need to make alternative arrangements."

"The more you do, the more you're worth."

This assumption sounds right, but it twists the truth by confusing external gain with individual value. It would be true to say, "The more you do, the more you accomplish," or, "The more you do, the more other people notice you." The assumption implies your value has to be earned. It doesn't. As a human being you have inherent worth. A more correct and loving message to give yourself would be: "I am worth a great deal, no matter what I accomplish."

"It's easier to do it myself."

Excuses are the toughest assumptions to crack because they are part of your defense system. Picture them as frontline soldiers protecting your indispensability. Excuses are often true, which is one reason it's hard to challenge them. So instead of trying to disprove them, question their usefulness in your life. For example, maybe it *is* easier to do it yourself. But isn't that how you end up doing more than your share? Rather than replacing the assumption entirely, try adding to it. For example, you might say, "It's easier for now to do it myself, but it makes life harder in the long run," or, "It's easier to do it myself, but I think I'll hold off this time and see what happens."

Identify one or two key assumptions underlying your indispensability and hold them up for questioning.

ROADBLOCKS

The main roadblock to examining assumptions is your own fear of letting go of beliefs that help you justify your perfectionism. If you start thinking about things differently, you may need to act differently!

The mind is incredibly tenacious. It will argue you out of every attempt to alter your assumptions. Changing the way you think is like repeatedly wrapping your finger around a strand of perfectly straight hair in the hope that it will hold a curl. Each time you release it, the hair falls stubbornly back into place. The same is true of your long-held assumptions.

PRACTICALLY SPEAKING...

Replacing old assumptions with updated ones is best done with the help of a mate or trusted friend (as long as that person is committed to your personal growth), within a support group, or with a professional counselor.

New assumptions must be reinforced through repetition. Saying them out loud several times a day is one way. Writing them down and taping them to your refrigerator or in a conspicuous place in your room is another. As you begin altering your assumptions, you will experience concrete rewards.

Like Karen, the high-strung manager of a busy car rental company, who realized the phrase "I can't afford to make mistakes" was underlying her behavior. Those words kept popping into her mind, especially when she was under a lot of stress. For several weeks, right before bed, Karen practiced repeating the phrase "I only have to do my best." To her delight, Karen began waking in the morning feeling calmer and more refreshed, instead of nervous and jittery. As she continued working on relinquishing perfectionistic assumptions for more positive ones, she felt increasingly less pressured and more accepting of herself.

STEP FOUR: GIVE YOURSELF PERMISSION TO ACKNOWLEDGE YOUR FEELINGS

You acknowledge your feelings when you are honest about them instead of suppressing them, censoring them, or pretending they don't exist. You reveal your vulnerabilities, rather than acting like a perfectly tuned machine that never breaks down. You accept your feelings as normal, and valid, and part of what makes you a unique and lovable human being.

You might say, "But of course I have feelings. Everyone has feelings!" What's meant here by "having feelings" goes beyond acknowledging that they exist; the process of giving yourself permission includes: EXPERIENCING, FACING, ACCEPTING, and EXPRESSING your emotions. Each is vitally important to beating the perfection addiction.

• EXPERIENCING emotions means feeling them in as pure and natural a fashion as possible. As we become older we learn to check any excess show of emotion. We can't differentiate between undue childish outbursts and healthy expressions of feelings. To cover and control ourselves, we begin to intellectualize and detach from our emotions—a way of putting *ourselves* over here and our *feelings* over there.

Detachment is denial's henchman. As long as you're cut off from feelings, you fool yourself that everything's all right. You go merrily along making yourself indispensable without realizing how drained or needy or resentful you are on the inside. Repressing feelings deprives you of valuable information as to the costs of your perfectionism. Allowing yourself to experience the full repertoire of feelings is necessary to know what needs to change.

• FACING your feelings means looking at what's underneath them. This is key to coming to terms because as recovery progresses, underlying issues emerge. Long-festering resentments and untended needs sprout up like insistent seedlings poking through virgin ground. Anger appears—at the years of setting aside your needs to cater to everyone else's. Sadness—at having to perform and prove yourself again and again. Fear—at the prospect of changing and learning a new way of being in the world. These feelings must be addressed and dealt with directly for resolution to occur.

• ACCEPTING your feelings—claiming them as a natural and intrinsic part of yourself—is essential. Being perfect means not having "bad" feelings. When bad, unacceptable, or dangerous feelings like anger, sadness, or fear creep in, they upset us. So we rationalize or bury them deep down where they won't make any more trouble.

It's essential to accept *all* your feelings. The woman who finds it impossible to say no to her mother—never mind that she's tired, or busy, or doesn't feel like responding—eventually begins to feel her mother is taking advantage of her. She feels angry and hostile, but pushes these feelings aside, telling herself, "I shouldn't be angry. I'm bad for even thinking that way." Once she's aware of and accepts her feelings of anger, she sees it's not possible, or even right, to expect herself to be an "on-call" daughter. To another woman, indispensability is her only weapon in battling the menacing childhood shadows of abandonment. If she could admit the fear, even in brief spurts, instead of frantically trying to escape it, she might be able to relax her expectations and accept her feelings instead of running away from them!

• EXPRESSING your feelings is crucial on a number of counts. Taking a deep breath and letting down the barriers penetrates painful isolation. When you are able to reveal your inner emotions— the unabridged version—you cross the distance that separates you from the rest of humanity.

Expressing your emotions transforms other people's expectations and paves the way for support. Saying how you feel is key to forming more equal and realistic relationships; how can people help or support you when they haven't a clue to how you're really doing?

There are countless opportunities, day in and day out, to practice expressing your feelings. Typical scene: You've been up since
six A.M., gotten the kids ready for school, put in a long, grueling
day at work, made dinner, and now you're ready to collapse.
You'd give anything to take a long hot bath, don your robe, put
your feet up, and thumb through a magazine. But the dinner dishes
are still on the table, the kids need help with their homework, there
are arrangements to be made for the neighborhood block party, the
checkbook needs balancing, and someone has to go to the grocery
store because you're running out of ingenious recipes starring noo-
dles, cream of mushroom soup, and frozen peas. You let out an
audible sigh. Your husband, getting up from the table, casually
mentions he's off to a game with the guys, he'll be back by ten.
This is a perfect opening. Do you stifle your anger, glance up
cheerfully, and say, "That's nice, honey. Have a good time," while
muttering under your breath, "Thanks a lot, jerk." Or do you say,
"I had a long day. I'm tired and I'm not up to handling everything
that has to be done. I'll be angry if you go out now. I need your
help."

Another scene, along the same vein: The past few weeks you've
been going through a rough time. You've been having problems
with your boyfriend and no one's been particularly understanding,
not even your best friend. You're down, depressed, you've been
stuffing food, you've gained weight, and all in all, you're feeling
just plain lousy about yourself. It's taking all your energy just to
maintain appearances at work. As you are about to leave the office,
your boss calls you in and says, "Ruth, I'm concerned. You know
how I count on you to keep up morale, but lately you just don't
seem to be putting your best foot forward. I don't know what's
wrong, but whatever it is, I hope you work it out soon."

This scenario is a little thornier. You fear jeopardizing your position. On the other hand, how long can you keep putting up a front
and acting like Pollyanna? Do you put on a happy face and tell your
boss, "Oh, it's nothing. I'm sure I'll be back to my old self by
tomorrow." Or, do you take this chance to be honest about what a
hard time you've been having and explain that right now you need
time to work through what's bothering you, and, by the way, you'd

appreciate your boss's support? If you take the risk and express your feelings, there is the chance you will begin to break down the perception of indispensability—of being someone who appears selfless and always ready to serve. For all you know, the other person may be wishing he or she could see your more human, more vulnerable side. Dismantling the image of Superwoman lets others in and permits them to give.

How to give yourself permission involves first changing your relationship with yourself, and then your relationships with others. It requires cutting through a long pattern of blocking, and ignoring, and diminishing your feelings to protect yourself from hurt. In return, you also free yourself to experience the positive feelings—joy, excitement, pleasure, and gratitude—which have been equally suppressed.

The confidence to be in your feelings requires a great deal of trust in yourself. It takes courage to share your emotions and put yourself unabashedly on the line.

ROADBLOCKS

Learning to experience, face, accept, and express feelings is difficult, especially for perfectionists who have become very accomplished at doing the opposite. Our culture teaches that expressing feelings is at best self-indulgent, at worst a serious handicap to success. Certainly, women have had a vast advantage over men in terms of being able to express their emotions without arousing scorn. But there's a twist: women are encouraged to express their emotions, but then they're either patronized or punished for doing so. Women who make themselves indispensable have learned this lesson very well.

Expressing feelings is threatening because we aren't supposed to have any. Not having feelings is one of the unspoken rules of indispensability; it's what frees us to take care of everyone else. If we experience and face our feelings, we find we are not always willing or able to accommodate others. If we accept and express our emotions, we have opened the door to acknowledging our needs.

There are definite costs to the honest expressing of emotions, especially in situations where doing so may bring up potentially explosive conflicts or threaten the status quo. Working this step might provoke the need to make changes in your life; you might find you must seriously analyze the long-term future of relationships or reevaluate your comfort with the level of emotional honesty sanctioned at work. Some relationships will flourish from your being more candid. In others, it might be wisest to continue censoring yourself or share your feelings a little at a time. Be selective and judicious in choosing where, how, and to whom you express your feelings. Take great care in protecting yourself.

PRACTICALLY SPEAKING...

You need to pay attention to your feelings. We are so conditioned to disregard and justify our emotional responses, it takes real effort to take note and take them seriously. Distraction is one typical way of discounting feelings. If you notice yourself looking for *anything* to do as an alternative to letting yourself experience your feelings (eating, chattering, rationalizing, shopping, working, and having sex are a few of the ways we distract ourselves), force yourself to stay in touch.

One concrete approach to accepting your feelings is to look at whether you're applying a double standard to yourself. When you catch yourself being judgmental or hard on yourself, think about how you treat the people you love. Is your affection limited to those times your friends or family members are feeling strong and seem to have it all together? Do you love them any less when they're hurting? Probably not. If anything, vulnerability makes them more human. Give yourself the same freedom you allow others.

* * *

This list of STOPs and STARTs provides concrete ways of unlearning old behavior and developing new ways of supporting your feelings:

Stop burying yourself in activity.
Start making time to hear and feel your feelings.

Stop cutting off feelings mid-stream.
Start allowing yourself to go all the way.

Stop rationalizing your feelings.
Start giving them serious consideration.

Stop justifying your feelings and trying to explain them.
Start accepting them.

Stop criticizing and punishing yourself for having "bad" feelings.
Start rewarding yourself for being honest.

Stop concealing your feelings.
Start sharing them.

STEP FIVE: IDENTIFY YOUR NEEDS

Identifying your needs *means* knowing what's essential for your health, happiness, and personal development. It means acknowledging you *have* needs and focusing on them, instead of being overly concerned with everyone else's. It means clarifying your most essential, bottom-line requirements, along with the specifics, and keeping up with them as they change.

As we saw in Chapter Five, the payoffs of perfectionism range from praise to promotions; from a spotless floor to a sense of belonging and security. Indispensability serves as a shortcut. When you stop the habitual behavior, you will feel empty. You must learn to identify and fulfill these needs in new, more direct ways.

For example, over many years, Nina put herself in the middle of family conflicts. Warm, empathetic, and level-headed, she took to the role naturally, and acting as referee made her feel needed and important. But she also felt like the rope in a game of tug-of-war.

Once Nina extricated herself from the middle, giving up her attempts to patch differences and "make" everyone get along, she realized her sadness that her family, like most, fell short of her fantasy. She also realized that her need to belong had led her into a thankless role. Nina was able to form new, more realistic relationships within her family and find other, more satisfying ways of using her gifts for arbitration and healing.

Trying to get your needs met through other people is faulty on two counts: It isn't their job to make you feel loved or needed, and you end up overly dependent on others as the source of your self-esteem.

Like Mitzi, who grew up on the "wrong side of the tracks," and pushed and pushed her boyfriend, who was struggling to get a fledgling business off the ground. Although she didn't have any accounting experience, Mitzi took over the books, sat in on sales calls, and called weekly meetings for Mark to report on his progress. Bent on marrying someone who would provide the lost security of her childhood, Mitzi set out to groom Mark for the role. While it appeared that Mitzi was calling the shots, after six months, Mark, tired of her pushiness, got rid of the business *and* her. Mitzi got the point. She went into therapy to deal with her insecurity and rebuild her identity on the basis of her own accomplishments.

Another woman, Elaine, who had been a painfully shy child and late-blooming adolescent, threw herself into motherhood with the energy and verve of an executive bent on reaching the top. She wore herself out dragging her children to dance, gymnastics, Suzuki music lessons, and French lessons, pushing them to make up for the success and popularity she had missed. Her goal: to have accomplished kids who felt like "real winners." Their response: anxiety and resentment at having to compete constantly. Instead of making herself indispensable to her children so as to enjoy vicariously their success (a strategy that generally backfires anyway), Elaine needed to learn how to get out there and make it happen for herself.

As you push your needs aside, they become increasingly blurred and obstructed, until you aren't able to delineate their shape. When someone asks, "What do you need?" the honest answer is "I don't know." Even the question feels overwhelming.

Identifying needs is important in that it's the first step toward acting on them. If you're not aware of your needs, you're more apt to pressure yourself and take on more than is reasonable. You can give and give and give without feeling like you're *really getting* what you came for. Putting your needs into the formula forces you to reevaluate your choices.

Identifying your needs also challenges the image you've promoted of yourself as totally self-sufficient and autonomous. By this time, you've convinced everyone you really *don't* need a thing! Even when you *do* admit needs, you're quick to negate them with comments like "But everything will be fine" and "It's no big deal." Clarifying your needs—for help, for reassurance, for security, comfort, and love—makes it harder to brush them off and sets the groundwork for asking for support. There are three steps to identifying your needs:

1. *Examine your motives.* Why are you making yourself indispensable? What needs are being fulfilled?

2. *Articulate your needs.* Say them out loud or write them in a notebook. Begin each sentence with "I need . . ." Notice how you feel each time you complete the sentence.

3. *Clarify.* Consider each need in depth. Think about what it means in your life. Look at whether it's a basic need—something fundamental to your well-being—or more fleeting and situa-

tional. Has it existed for a long time, or has it developed more recently?

The idea of considering your needs, when you haven't been oriented that way, may seem hopelessly overwhelming. It needn't be if you follow these three steps in a way that works for you.

For Lucy, what was most effective was sitting down with a friend and reeling off everything she needed (no holds barred) while the friend took notes. She came up with dozens, everything from needing more sleep to needing help with the yardwork to needing a thank-you when she did something for her children. Next, her friend read the list back to Lucy and had her assign a rank to each on the basis of how essential it was to her health, productivity, and well-being. As they discussed each need, Lucy gained insight about what was really important in her life and was soon able to begin thinking in terms of satisfying her needs.

ROADBLOCKS

Needs and indispensability seem mutually exclusive. The very notion of considering personal needs meets with a number of immediate objections:

I don't have time to think about my needs!
and

My needs are nothing compared to other people's.
and

Why worry about my needs? I have better things to do.

Each of these statements is a handicap. But then, as an Indispensable Woman, diminishing your needs is a long-established pattern. Like most women, you have been taught to subjugate or downplay your needs in order to be "nice" and "thoughtful" and "caring" and "giving." It takes conscious effort to form a new image of yourself as a good person with needs.

Seeing needs as a roadblock to achievement is an example of a realistic obstacle blown out of proportion. Identifying your needs might indeed slow you down and limit what you can accomplish. However, the overriding goals of health, happiness, and personal fulfillment allow you to integrate achievements into the total picture of your life and appreciate them more fully.

One final roadblock to identifying needs is the fear of discovering they aren't being met. Looking at your needs squarely requires the courage to confront the areas of your life that require attention and work.

PRACTICALLY SPEAKING...

1. Make a shopping list of your needs. Write each one down separately with the intention of finding out how to meet it. Update the list on a frequent basis.

2. Put yourself in a position where it's impossible to respond to anyone else's needs. Go away for a couple of days or simply call a moratorium. Be aware of how you feel when you aren't being indispensable. What do *you* want? What do *you* need?

3. Don't act like the "Reality Police." For example, when you say, "I need time for myself," don't intervene with comments like "But there isn't any," or "Where will I get it?" Countering needs with objections stops you short. State your needs as if you fully expect to fulfill them.

4. Ask someone who knows you very well to tell you what he or she thinks you need. Note if this person identifies areas you've missed.

5. When you're feeling anxious or down in the dumps, ask yourself what you need. When you're feeling happy and content, ask yourself what you're getting.

STEP SIX: SIMPLIFY

Simplifying is scaling back. When you simplify your life you divest yourself of some of your responsibilities by deciding what you really *do* and *don't* have to do. It's a little like cleaning your closet. It's hard to throw anything away (it doesn't seem possible you'll survive without that fabulous orange paisley shirt you found three summers ago at the basement bargain sale. Of course you're still looking for the perfect skirt to go with it!), but getting rid of it is the only way to create space, or in this case, breathing room.

As we've seen, having too much responsibility isn't the sole cause of your pressure. But that doesn't mean it isn't a major contributing factor. Internal shifts that change the general way you look at your life aren't enough unless you also address the specifics. Step six is about making specific, concrete changes *today* that help you become less indispensable and reduce your stress.

Simplifying your life is important on several counts. First, no matter how much you talk about wishing your life would slow down, everything remains status quo until you are willing to act. If you keep doing the lion's share of the housework, no matter how loudly you complain, nothing will change until you stop performing and start negotiating. If you continue allowing yourself to be pressured and intimidated by an employer who is at least as perfectionistic as you (it's plenty hard to breeze out of the office at five when your boss is just settling in for the evening), your life won't be your own, now or in the future.

As long as you're up to your ears in obligations, it's impossible to see what needs to change. It's a bit of a catch-22. You have to make the first move, putting some perceptible dent in your existing habits, in order to push through the clutter and gain any clarity.

A few years ago, Gary and I hired a regular Thursday night babysitter so we could get out and have a little grown-up time once each week. Every Thursday night, regardless of what was going on or how I was feeling, we would rush out at 6:30, even though the children didn't get home from day-care until almost six.

One Thursday night, after a particularly difficult day writing, one of those days when nothing seemed to flow, we went to one of our favorite restaurants. We'd just ordered dinner, and Gary was trying to tell me about something important that had happened at work, when I realized I just couldn't listen. My heart was back at home. All I could think of was how much I missed the kids and wished I were in my jeans, sitting on the couch, reading them books and getting them settled down for bed. I looked across the table and said, "I'm sorry, honey, but I just realized I really don't want to be here."

"But it's Thursday night," he replied. "We have a babysitter and you're all dressed up, and besides, the dinner is almost here."

Just then, the waiter served our meals.

"Could I please have a doggie bag?" I asked, by this time determined to leave. When we got home, I realized something important: my evening out had become just another appointment on my itinerary. Instead of being tuned in to what I wanted and needed, I was going through life like a sleepwalker. Right then, I made a decision to pay better attention to myself, instead of letting my schedule dictate my life.

Simplifying is important to create or restore balance. Being stuck in a particular way of doing things, you may not notice how little rest you get, or that you aren't making time for friendship, or that exercise has taken a real back seat. Relinquishing some of your responsibility frees you to cultivate other aspects of life— activities and interests that round you out and provide self-nurturing and perspective.

Finally, making changes—and seeing concrete results—gives you confidence and hope that further change is possible. It is exhilarating to observe the rewards of taking charge of your own life. Each positive move toward making yourself less indispensable makes the next step easier. And changes in one area of your life easily transfer to other parts.

For example, Susan, the advertising executive from Chapter One whose need to be noticed was destroying her work life, home life, and health, took the step of asking her supervisor at work for help on a project instead of faking her way through in order to maintain her image as someone who always had the answers. The few hours Susan and her supervisor spent together working on the project yielded noticeable rewards: Susan received the guidance she needed, increased her knowledge, and began to forge a more personal relationship with her supervisor, who up until that point had taken her cues from Susan and kept her distance. And, having had such a positive experience, Susan started making tentative requests of her husband Rick as well, asking his advice, and letting him comfort and support her.

Any improvements in the routines or relationships that reflect your indispensability are worthwhile. The hardest part is knowing where to start. *How* to go about simplifying is to go through the various aspects of your life and identify specific problems that cause stress.

Each person's problem areas—or pressure points—are different. For some women, indispensability is manifested most at work; others have the hardest time at home or in personal relationships.

Think about the actual times when you are most aware of being in a state of overload. What, for you, are the incidents that either set up or intensify stress? For instance, at home, are your mornings the most tumultuous period (you're exhausted before you've even stepped out the door), or does everything converge, like a traffic jam, at the end of the day? Are there certain times in your job when tension is greatest, say, when important deadlines are approaching or when your employer is out of town? Try to determine when the pressure points are at their most intense.

Once you've narrowed down when you're most likely to get stressed out, it's time to make concrete changes. What can *you* do to simplify your responsibilities in these situations?

Let's say you discover that the most stressful time at home is the dinner hour, when you've just come in the door, need to change clothes, read the mail, make dinner, and deal with your children. What are your alternatives? Perhaps your mate needs to be actively responsible for the kids for that period of time. Or maybe you need a fifteen-minute breather, upstairs alone in your room to help ease the transition. Or maybe you need a crock pot or a stock of frozen dinners in the freezer.

Maybe the majority of your stress originates at work. Is there a way to restructure your job description, building in a little more flexibility? What about delegating, organizing, figuring out which projects are the most urgent, and seeing if you can give up a few that are less crucial to your reputation and future career moves? Have you chosen to work in a high-pressure environment where sixty hours a week is the norm? Do you need to rethink your choices, or is it possible to be a trailblazer and change the system? One woman, realizing there wasn't a way to reduce her work load, compromised by "scheduling her stress." She decided to add an extra hour on each side of her weekdays and completely stopped coming in on the weekends.

Simplifying also involves looking at ways to lessen your stress by changing your expectations of yourself. Think about ways you either create or add to the pressure in your life. Do you jump up and do the dishes or answer the phone before anyone else has a chance? Have you locked yourself into spending two hours every night helping your child with homework, no matter what else you need to do? Have you given your friends carte blanche to call on you when they need you, without spelling out any conditions?

A lot of simplifying can be done if you are willing to be honest with other people about what you will and won't do. To do so, you must also change your attitude. Everything seems urgent when you are ruled by inner tension and anxiety. When perfectionism is the standard, it doesn't matter how many actual tasks you let go of—you quickly fill the void with new demands.

For this reason, it's very important to reinforce giving up responsibilities by building in positive steps to reduce your stress. It's helpful to set up a specific part of each and every day for relaxation; you might take a short period each morning to sit quietly or meditate. Or set aside a half hour each night before bed to read or listen to a relaxation tape. If you can afford it, a body massage can be a real treat and make a difference in how you feel. Exercise and recreational sports also can be great for inner relaxation, as long as you don't get hooked into competing. I find that a hot, candlelit bath does wonders to lessen stress. Whatever you do, these relaxation methods need to be built into your life on a regular basis, given as firm a priority as your tasks and obligations. If it helps, schedule them in.

ROADBLOCKS

There are two big roadblocks to simplifying your life. First, finding a place to start scaling back seems close to impossible. You're so entrenched in all your responsibilities, it's hard to see any way out.

There is a way out, and that's a little at a time. Small changes are all that's called for; it isn't necessary to put your life through an entire overhaul. Just take one thing at a time. One change will lead to another.

You may also feel resistance to the idea of simplifying your life. You may fear that if you start giving up responsibilities, you'll end up without enough to do. You may be concerned that if you alter your relationships too much, no one will need you or you'll end up alone. You may think that the level of pressure you experience is proof of having a full, exciting, satisfying existence.

It isn't. In fact, by simplifying your life, you are able to stop squandering your energy and be more focused, clearheaded, and relaxed. Instead of spreading yourself thin, you can devote yourself to what really matters, what's most important in your life.

PRACTICALLY SPEAKING...

The only way to simplify your life is to start making changes. Do whatever helps you to take action, whether it's asking friends to support you, making lists and crossing resolutions off once they've been accomplished, or giving yourself rewards for positive changes.

I asked ten women to share the first step they took toward simplifying their lives. This is what they said:

"I turned down a promotion at work that would have been a third more money and ten times the aggravation."

"I agreed to let my eight-year-old pick out her own clothes for school."

"I stopped sending birthday cards to my husband's side of the family."

"I bought a microwave."

"I referred my best friend to a therapist."

"I resigned from two committees."

"I started using paper plates."

"I hired an older woman to live with us and help with the kids."

"I learned to always count to five before responding."

"I got a DO NOT DISTURB sign for my bedroom door."

There are lots of rewards that come your way once you start making changes. One woman talked happily of waking in the morning rested. Another noticed that her employer and boss began treating her more respectfully when she started taking better care of herself. Another shared the following reactions:

"I was pretty nervous when I sat down with my husband and told him I'd had enough of doing everything, that it was time to start sharing responsibilities. But once we talked and really divided things up, he and I both felt much better. He said he'd felt left out, especially when it came to cooking and taking care of the children. He was glad to help, and since then we've done lots more together, which I feel has brought us closer. There's less tension and more cooperation."

Not everyone reacts this way. Once you begin making changes, you may encounter opposition and anger. Those individuals who have been the primary beneficiaries of your caretaking and indispensability may bristle at your efforts to shed some of your burden. There is no way to predict or control others' reactions. You can prepare yourself if, ahead of time, you carefully scrutinize each change you are considering making, asking yourself these questions:

What do I want to change?

How badly do I want to change it?

What are the potential rewards?

Is there any possible backlash?

If so, can I accept what comes?

If you know, in your heart, that the changes you are setting out to make will simplify your life and make it possible to lead a happier, more balanced existence, that conviction will serve you well in knowing what's right to do.

STEP SEVEN: SEEK SUPPORT

Seeking support starts with giving up the notion you can do it all by yourself. It means communicating your needs. It means reaching out and recruiting people who will assist, encourage, and champion your recovery.

Support is defined as

Cooperation

Physical assistance of any sort

Nonjudgmental feedback and encouragement

Anything that helps you get your needs met and restores balance to your life.

Actively seeking support is important in a number of ways. Consistent and ongoing support improves the chances for positive and enduring change. If you've ever tried to make major changes in your life, you know how much difference it makes when there's someone to count on for reassurance and positive reinforcement. Having someone to talk to and try out ideas with, someone who will gently nudge you when necessary, applaud your progress and encourage you when the going gets tough, is of utmost importance.

Learning to initiate and to accept help when it's offered is a necessary skill for the recovering Indispensable Woman to cultivate. There is a little girl in each and every one of us who needs to be held and nurtured and taken care of. In order to succeed at making ourselves indispensable, it was a matter of survival to renounce that little girl in favor of being utterly self-sufficient and "grown up." Real maturity demands we embrace our younger selves, the awkward, shy, needy part of ourselves that hungers for support and is gratefully receptive. Seeking support is proof we no longer expect ourselves to be perfect.

There are two sides to seeking support: ASKING for support and ALLOWING it in.

First, you must ask for what you need. This requires honest communication (stray hints, wishful thinking, or beating around the bush don't count!) and being as specific as possible. "HELP!!!" is a good opening line; "I need you to come over three weeks from Saturday from 9:30 until noon to help me move furniture to my new apartment" is much more to the point. If you've had a hard time asking for support in the past, you may assume everyone will jump once you say the word. Realistically, it's best to also be prepared for the possibility of being turned down.

Once you've asked for support, being open and responsive is *your* responsibility. Often, we have a hard time accepting support. We're too proud or embarrassed or defensive to really take it in. Either the support isn't offered in exactly the form we were looking for, or we're afraid that by letting it in, we'll turn into a blubbering mass of needs. Taking in support means opening your mind to the possibility that people are ready to help. And opening your heart enough to let them in.

Early on in writing this book, I learned an important lesson about allowing support in. Being an Indispensable Woman, I made the mistake of agreeing to an impossibly short deadline. "Sure," I said eagerly, "I'll get it done, no problem." Two months into the process, I sent in a first draft. My editor's response was a phone call saying, "This has a long way to go. It needs a lot of work." I was devastated. But I wasn't really surprised that the manuscript had problems. I knew I was under terrible pressure. I wasn't eating or sleeping well. I was barking at Gary and the kids. Each day I'd sit at my computer, the kitchen clock boring a hole in my back, feeling as if I were running a marathon, trying desperately to make it to the finish line.

When the call from my editor came, for the first time I let myself really feel my fear. Maybe I had bitten off more than I could chew. Maybe this once I couldn't deliver. I saw that I couldn't keep going on the same way. I realized I needed support. And, because I wanted so much to be able to continue, I reached out and asked for help. I called friends and asked for their reassurance that I had what it takes to complete the project. I called a woman I'd met, a well-known writer, and asked her to be a mentor, and share her greater experience and wisdom. I called my editor and asked for an extension. It took me ten days to get up the nerve to ask for it. It took five minutes to work out the arrangements. Wherever I turned, everyone was right there, more than willing to help. That was the easy part. The hard part was letting myself accept it. I had to work at not dismissing my friends' positive reinforcement. I had to swallow my pride in order to make real use of the guidance I was given. And even when the extension was granted, I still had to fight the urge to play "beat the deadline."

SPIRITUAL SUPPORT

Acknowledging the need for support goes hand in hand with giving up control, which can be a frightening proposition. Once we admit our lives are out of control, that we are not the center of the universe, that we have unresolved feelings and unmet needs, once we take responsibility for our own recovery and are willing to say, "Okay, I'm not in control of everything, I can see I'm not really indispensable," *what then?* Coming to grips with the truth sends us reeling into a new reality. Before, we felt in control. Uncertainty and confusion seem the new, not very comforting landmarks of recovery. What to do now? Where to turn?

Thus far, we have been talking about seeking support from other individuals. But there is a whole realm of spiritual energy and solace that cannot be stressed enough as a source of enduring support. Whether you nourish your need for spiritual comfort and connection through solitude, poetry, prayer, fellowship, or something else, support also includes reaching out for spiritual guidance and nourishing your soul.

ROADBLOCKS

Self-image and fear are major roadblocks to seeking support. For many women, asking for help is tantamount to admitting failure. Saying "I need support" translates into "Something's wrong with me and everyone's going to find out." Being perceived as someone with "problems" threatens the Indispensable Woman's ego.

Fear of the unknown is another serious obstacle to seeking support. We hesitate to embark into uncharted territory; being novices at reaching out, we are afraid of what we might find. Emptiness, isolation, and emotional bankruptcy might need to be confronted in the pursuit of spiritual support.

We fear rejection most of all. As long as we take care of ourselves and don't ask too much of anyone, we are safe. Once we ask, we take a gamble. We risk rejection, but also stand a chance of getting what we need.

PRACTICALLY SPEAKING...

Seeking support takes practice and *does* get easier with time. Some tangible tips:

Join or start a support group. Seek out other women with a shared interest in learning how to stop pressuring themselves to be perfect. Run a want ad or post a sign at work, at the neighborhood grocery store, the mall, at your church or synagogue, or anywhere else women are likely to notice.²

Make a commitment to ask for support once each day. It doesn't have to be anything huge—asking for a hug or five minutes of someone's time is just fine.

Find a poem, scriptural passage, or other inspirational reading and read it daily.

Each time you do something nice for someone, follow it up by doing something nice for yourself.

Surround yourself with people who support your recovery. Try to avoid anyone who manipulates, pressures, or encourages you to make yourself indispensable.

Make quality time for yourself. This time should be reserved for activities that rejuvenate your energy and bolster your self-esteem: attend an interesting lecture, read a good book, make a wonderful meal and enjoy it with a friend, get some fresh air and exercise (just for fun), take a nap, make love, or pamper yourself with a haircut, warm bath, manicure, massage, or special shopping trip. Work isn't permitted. Set aside regular, scheduled time each day and stick to it. Whether it's fifteen minutes or two hours, make it sacred.

STEP EIGHT: LET GO OF GUILT

Letting go of guilt begins with accepting that you are human and therefore limited in what you can give. It means silencing the relentless inner voice criticizing you for not being better and doing more. It means you stop berating yourself for what you *can't* do and feel good about what you *can*.

It's important to let go of guilt because hanging on to it keeps us mired in our indispensability. When we fall short of our expectations, we feel bad and anxious and ashamed. Guilt is the punishment we mete out to ourselves for not being perfect. (How could I have screwed up? I should do better than that!) It is the basis on which we monitor our behavior (I feel guilty. I'm not doing enough.), and the scale on which we balance and judge our performance. (Not up to snuff—better do more!)

We make ourselves crazy over the slightest infraction and worry ourselves sick over anything left undone. We agonize over potential disaster and are mercilessly unforgiving when we fall short of the mark. The only way to feel better is by doing more, and so the cycle of indispensability is reenacted again and again.

Learning to let go of guilt improves the quality of our lives. Without persistent remorse pounding like a hammer inside our heads, eating away at us, we are clearer and more focused. Our judgment improves, we are more able to take pride in our accomplishments, celebrate our successes, and be grateful for what is good and right with the world.

Letting go of guilt is also critical in learning to stop managing and controlling other people's lives. In *Necessary Losses,* author Judith Viorst describes "omnipotent guilt" as stemming from the delusion that we have absolute power over the well-being of our loved ones.[3] Letting go of guilt doesn't mean abdicating responsibility or no longer caring. It does mean giving up responsibility for that which is beyond our control.

Guilt, when we are prisoners of it, feels the same regardless of its source. However, there are three distinct kinds of guilt: JUSTIFIED GUILT; IRRATIONAL GUILT; and SECOND-HAND GUILT.

Justified guilt describes feelings of remorse that are commensurate to damage done. You feel guilty either because someone has genuinely been hurt, because you really *could* have done better, or both.

Perfectionists find it terribly difficult to accept mistakes and grant ourselves forgiveness; we torment ourselves with "what ifs," retracing our every move, as if unlocking the mysterious answer as to where we went wrong will instantly reverse the outcome and prevent future transgressions.

Justified guilt, when it comes from having realistically failed ourselves or someone we care about, is relative to the magnitude of the crime. The missed phone call to cancel the dental appointment causes fleeting regret. The long-talked-about visit to an out-of-town, ailing grandparent that never materialized—and now it's too late—provokes unbearable anguish: How could I have been so selfish? How will I ever live with myself?

Forgiveness is the key. Letting go of justified guilt means acknowledging your error or shortcoming and expressing your repentance, without wallowing in self-recrimination. Letting go means putting what happened behind you—seeing the "what ifs" as circular and unproductive, learning from your experience and looking toward the future with greater insight and wisdom.

When you automatically blame yourself for everything that goes wrong in your life, you're experiencing irrational guilt. It's your fault. Whether or not you had anything to do with it. Whether or not you meant to hurt anyone. Whether or not you could, in reality, have helped it. Irrational means there isn't any good reason for feeling guilty, but that doesn't stop you from wallowing in it.

Like when your mate is suddenly moody and unresponsive and you're positive it's something you said. Or the political candidate you work for loses. Or your child doesn't get invited to the birthday party. Or your cat won't eat. Or . . .

Irrational guilt has two forms: OBSESSIVE AGONIZING, when you persist in beating your head against the wall, and FREE-FLOATING ANXIETY, the perpetual sensation of guilt that randomly attaches itself to anything in its path. Letting go of either seems an overwhelming task. These five points help get it down to size:

Figure out when you feel guilty.

How do you get hooked into guilt? Do you experience it most with your mother, your children, your boss? Does guilt come up in situations when you're feeling rushed? When you feel as if you haven't done your best? When you have to say no? Specifying how and when you feel most guilty makes it more tangible.

Stop the shoulds.

Cut off the insistent, demanding voice telling you what you "should" do. Typical "shoulds" are "Shouldn't you have known that?" "You should have done more." These kinds of judgments foster guilt and interfere with your efforts to let it go. Answer "shoulds" with "Why?" "Who says?" "I'm choosing not to."

Assess your responsibility.

Decide if your guilt is valid. Find out whether your anxiety is appropriate, whether your feelings of obligation are based in reality. Assessing your responsibility might reveal the need to take concrete action *or* you may find you are doing everything possible given your options and constraints.

Revise your expectations.

Once you've clarified your responsibility, alter your expectations accordingly. Stop blaming yourself and close the gap between what you "should" do and what is realistic.

Make peace.

Making peace is a process of reconciling perfection with reality. Coming to terms with the truth—that we are human beings with finite energy and resources; human beings who, despite the best of intentions, make mistakes, can't foresee the future, and aren't always one hundred percent—helps us accept we are doing our best.

It isn't easy to judge whether your feelings of guilt are well-grounded or exaggerated, as Jill found when she tried to assess her responsibility in a very trying situation. When Jill's father had a stroke, her mother made it clear she expected her daughter to make the trip cross country to be at her side. Jill, who had just been promoted to a new position in her company, told her mother she'd come home for the weekend, but that was all the time she could afford to be away. Her mother, who had offered to pay for the ticket, informed her she could come for a week, or not come at all. Jill said she'd buy her own ticket, which only angered her mother more.

Jill decided to stay in touch with the hospital long distance and forgo the trip. Being the only daughter, Jill felt as if she'd let her parents down. She knew she had made the best decision under the circumstances and was determined not to be manipulated, but she still felt heavy with guilt.

I suggested Jill ask herself the following questions:

Why am I feeling responsible?

Is there anything more I can do?

If so, what?

After much soul searching, Jill reached the conclusion that she really was living up to her responsibility. For her, making peace meant accepting she couldn't please her mother *and* maintain her own integrity. It took time, but she became comfortable with the necessary compromise.

Second-hand guilt is the guilt we take on from other people.

Although trying to get rid of the legacy of guilt from our parents is a central theme in most therapeutic work, and the phrase "Don't lay a guilt trip on me" has become part of the vernacular, the truth is *no one makes you feel guilty*. Other people may ask you to do more than you can, they may imply you have let them down or even openly complain of feeling neglected or hurt, but *you* aren't responsible for *their* feelings. When you establish boundaries and feel good about yourself, you're more able to see other people as separate human beings who are responsible for themselves. When you feel insecure about what you are able to give, you pick up every stray bit of guilt that comes your way.

ROADBLOCKS

Guilt is tricky because we confuse it with caring. Although we moan about our guilt as if it were a millstone, we consider it proof of our devotion. We measure our commitment in terms of our culpability, secretly patting ourselves on the back for caring enough to worry.

Guilt statements are often double messages. The woman who cancels an appointment saying, "I could kick myself for leaving you in the lurch," is also expressing her self-importance. Feeling guilty for disappointing our loved ones can be a way of proving how much we love them.

Another obstacle to liberating ourselves from guilt is that it alleviates the pain of living with our limitations. A young mother hires a well-trained nanny to take care of her new baby and then spends most of her time at work feeling guilty about leaving the child. An overworked executive finally takes a week's vacation, but can't relax because she's so busy worrying about being away. A grown woman, with a family of her own, is wracked with guilt for neglecting her eighty-year-old mother whom she is supporting in a nursing home three hundred miles away. For each, feeling guilty helps them feel better about not being able to be in two places at once. It reassures them of their commitment and connection. It softens the separation. It's the next best thing to being there.

PRACTICALLY SPEAKING...

Feeling guilty is a powerful ingrained response, one that can only be unlearned a little at a time. You will need to be especially patient with yourself during this step of recovery.

Affirmations are extremely useful in letting go of guilt. Creating positive statements to counteract the "shoulds" strips them of their power. Create an affirmation of your own that supports you in accepting more human expectations, or repeat one of the following:

"I am only responsible for what I can realistically accomplish."

"All my efforts are valuable."

"I am doing the best I can."

Another exercise I find helpful is what I call the "time test." This is how it works: Concentrate on one thing you are presently feeling guilty about. Now, ask yourself these questions: How much will this matter tomorrow? In three weeks? Six months? A year? Five years? Getting perspective on the immediate urgency either motivates you to make changes or helps relieve the guilt.

STEP NINE: SEE THE HUMOR

Seeing the humor means lightening up and laughing at yourself. It means not taking things so seriously—not seeing everything as a matter of life and death. It means being more tolerant of your mistakes, your pitfalls, and your shortcomings.

Humor is important in pulling you out of yourself. By humor, I mean gentle, light-hearted poking fun, not the cynical, sarcastic, self-deprecating put-downs women often use to dramatize or justify being overworked and unappreciated.

Humor is one of the first things to go when you're making yourself indispensable. The last thing you can see is how ridiculous you're being. (What's so funny about having a notebook next to my bed just in case I wake up in the middle of the night and think of something that needs to be done? I don't see anything silly about taping a picture of myself inside my daughter's lunch-box so she doesn't forget what I look like!) Recognizing the ways in which your perfectionism is funny, even ludicrous, lessens the intensity with which everything, including change, is approached.

When you can see the humor, you realize life isn't so deadly serious as you make it. Your frantic running around appears slightly slapstick; your efforts to control seem outrageous. Knowing that nothing is *that* important allows you to make more reasonable choices and commitments; seeing the absurdities makes it easier to forgive yourself when you fail.

Having a sense of humor is essential to accepting a more human image of yourself. You're more willing to back off and give yourself a little breathing room. Cultivating humor tears down the wall of isolation you've built around yourself. With laughter comes empathy and with empathy, self-acceptance.

Some ways *how* to see the humor in situations are:

Look at things in retrospect

It's almost impossible to see the humor in the moment. Most things look much funnier after the fact. Like the time you stayed up until dawn trying to clean the bathtub because your in-laws were coming to visit. You'd practically scrubbed off your skin before you realized you were trying to scrape off the caulking. Or the time you came in on the weekend thinking you'd surprise your boss and finish a project by Monday. But Monday was Labor Day. The office was closed. Or the time you spent hours before your child's birthday party decorating twenty-two rice cakes with shredded carrot hair, raisin eyes, banana noses, and apple mouths and then all the kids ate were potato chips. None of which seemed the least bit funny at the time!

Step outside yourself

Imagine looking at yourself through someone else's eyes. Or fantasize your life as a movie, with Lily Tomlin or Carol Burnett in the lead.

See the irony

Think about what you hope to gain by making yourself indispensable. Notice how often you end up with egg on your face, or achieving the exact opposite of what you set out to do.

Let other people in

Share the details of your perfectionism with other people. They're more likely to recognize and point out the humor. This doesn't mean setting yourself up to be laughed at, embarrassed, or made a fool of. Be sure to choose people you can trust to be loving and supportive.

ROADBLOCKS

The biggest obstacles to seeing the humor are being too busy, too isolated, and taking ourselves too seriously.

Not having enough time to laugh sounds absurd, but to many women it's a very serious problem. Humor seems like a waste of time, a sidetrack to achieving goals. Laughter requires letting down and relaxing, which we fight like swallowing bitter medicine.

In our isolation we become increasingly removed from seeing ourselves in relation to others. Without perspective nothing appears amusing, least of all ourselves.

Taking ourselves too seriously prevents us from accepting our flaws and our foibles. Our intense investment in an image of perfection makes it difficult to let down our guard and express our more playful and comical side.

PRACTICALLY SPEAKING...

These are some suggestions for cultivating humor:

Do something outrageous, something that requires spontaneity and shedding your inhibitions.

Share the account of an incident of making yourself indispensable that in retrospect seems ridiculous. Laugh about it.

Learn a few jokes and tell them to your friends.

Question: How many Indispensable Women does it take to change a lightbulb?

Answer: Three. One to write detailed instructions. One to change the lightbulb. And one to make sure it's done right.

See yourself as the cat in *The Cat in the Hat*⁴—holding a cup and a cake, two books and the fish and a little toy ship and some milk on a dish—all of which you've picked up with your own two hands!

If you have children, ask them to describe you.

Watch a funny movie or TV show (*Tootsie,* Charlie Chaplin, or *I Love Lucy* are terrific).

STEP TEN: CREATE REACHABLE GOALS

Reachable goals are those that are based on realistic expectations of success.

Creating reachable goals means basing your expectations on both your strengths and weaknesses. It means protecting your energy and establishing respectful and healthy boundaries. It means not promising more than you can deliver.

It's important to create new, more realistic goals because as long as you keep operating as if you can do it all, that is exactly what everyone expects of you. And you expect it of yourself. Reachable goals take *your* needs into account too! This doesn't mean slacking off or lowering your standards; what's important is to give yourself the best shot at successfully meeting your objectives. Perfectionists are overly optimistic about what can be accomplished in a day, forever playing catch up and feeling bad when anything's left undone. Set your sights on what is achievable and you vastly increase your likelihood of success, which, in turn, increases positive feelings about yourself.

There are two main skills needed for creating reachable goals: PRIORITIZING and SETTING LIMITS.

Prioritizing involves homing in on specific interests and talents, and making choices about what matters most and in what order.

Knowing what is important to you, both short-term and in the long run, enables you to create meaningful goals. Many people find it helpful to clarify values by putting them in writing. For example: "Having a career is critical to my self-esteem" or, "I care deeply about poverty in my community." Next, you need to translate values into goals. For example, "I will concentrate most of my effort into developing my career." Or, "I will make a commitment to work actively on easing poverty."

Home in by narrowing the choices. What are your skills? Talents? Areas of expertise? Is your time and energy spent in ways that maximize your creativity? Are you making the most of your gifts? What concrete goals will move you closer to getting what you want and need? Once you've homed in, within each goal there is the need to prioritize. That means making choices about what you can and cannot do, each and every day of your life. Since everything feels equally pressing, learning to make choices is complicated. What do you do when it's Saturday afternoon and you could go shopping (the cupboards are bare), see a friend (it's been a least a month), wash the kitchen floor (you're sticking to it), or sleep? (Heavens!) In the midst of a work crisis, you get calls from your mother, your fourteen-year-old daughter, and your best friend, all wanting something. How do you decide where to turn your attention first?

Here are questions to aid you in ordering your priorities.

Is it something that can wait? For how long?

Is there anyone else who can do it or help? Have you asked?

Could you do part of it? Is there a way to do it differently so it will take less time and energy?

Do you feel obligated or does it feel like a choice?

Will doing it satisfy your needs and make you feel good, or will it cause exhaustion and stress?

* * *

Once you've established your priorities, setting up boundaries is crucial for attaining your goals. The best intentions aren't good enough unless you learn to protect your energy by deciding what you have to give and then sticking with it. Saying, "This is as far as I'll go," and then hedging or giving in won't do. You have to be consistent and firm, or you undermine yourself. Healthful boundaries require being assertive with others. Saying no is the most blatant way to communicate limits, but there is quite a lot of gray area as well. Saying "Not now," or "I would be happy to do this much," and being very specific about your terms, are also options.

When you first start setting boundaries, there's a danger of coming on too strong. After being passive for so long, it's natural to be overly vehement in asserting your needs. Over time, you'll become more gracious in how you express yourself. Being respectful means having regard for other people's feelings and taking them into account too.

Finally, it's important to be flexible. Rigid expectations—holding on to ideas that are unchallengeable, plans carved in stone, or paths no longer productive—work counter to reaching goals and create unnecessary pressure. Goals must be updated. Priorities change, and new circumstances dictate the need to adapt. Keeping your awareness in the present is the best way to stay flexible. One sure test: When you suspect you're being rigid, ask yourself: Is this something I want and need to be doing *right now*? Is there *another* way to look at things? (If you suspect you're being rigid, ask for feedback. This is one thing people around us are generally quick to spot.)

ROADBLOCKS

Perfectionism distorts reality, making it very difficult to discern between realistic goals and compulsive overachievement. With perfectionism as the standard, no goal can ever be fully realized. The need for external validation—how do I decide what's enough without someone else saying?—makes it patently impossible to judge and appreciate our success.

There are specific obstacles in the path of creating reachable goals:

Clarifying values: The Indispensable Woman, used to being absorbed with others, isn't accustomed to concentrating on what matters in her *own* life or to thinking long-term.

Prioritizing: To perfectionists, prioritizing automatically implies failure in those areas that must be put off or set aside.

Setting Limits: The single greatest challenge! Establishing boundaries profoundly threatens our indispensability. Losing face, losing ground, losing security, and losing love are but a few of the fears of drawing lines.

Flexibility: Finally, our investment in being in control makes it hard to be adaptable and relaxed about what happens. Flexibility forces us to look to both sides instead of straight ahead, and when necessary, realign our focus and direction.

PRACTICALLY SPEAKING...

Achieving your goals includes doing anything that furthers your commitment to stop making yourself indispensable. The likelihood of reaching new, nonperfectionistic goals rests on the ongoing pursuit of the practical suggestions included in all ten steps of recovery.

Specific tips for creating more reachable goals include:

- **Don't say yes unless you are sure you can follow through.**

- Always give yourself more time than you need.

- Don't do it for them if they can do it themselves.

- Enforce mandatory rest, relaxation, and rewards for yourself.

- Take your phone off the hook.

- Practice the art of closing your eyes and letting the dishes, the laundry, the closets sit.

- Say "No."

- Judge yourself with the same compassion you afford others.

- Accept yourself as someone who is changing.

- Be patient.

NINE

SMALL STEPS

Recovery is a slow, gradual process. It is a journey of putting one foot in front of the other. It requires making a long-term investment and being satisfied with small, significant progress rather than immediate, total transformation.

Perfectionists, true to form, approach change with sky-high expectations. (Tell me what's wrong and I'll fix it. Yesterday! Perfectly!) Expecting too much, too soon, creates undue pressure and is a way of setting yourself up to fail. *There is no such thing as a perfect recovery.* Each and every individual encounters stumbling blocks and barriers along the way.

Like a child beginning to walk, improving the quality of your life is a series of starts and stops. A toddler doesn't stand up for the first time and stride confidently across the room. First she crawls, then tiptoes around furniture, holding on for dear life, then totters forward, falters, falls, and begins again. The tumbles are a necessary part of the learning process.

I hope you will experience a minimum of setbacks and a steady string of recognizable successes. However, it's natural, after making yourself indispensable for so long, to fall back into old, familiar modes. Even those women with the most fervent intentions of "sticking to the program" occasionally revert to prior compulsive patterns.

SLIPS

A slip is any unintentional behavior motivated by perfectionism or indispensability. Some general categories of slips are

Overloading your schedule

Taking on more than you can realistically handle

Compulsive activity

Being fixated on finishing a project (large or small)

Tuning out other people's feedback

Neglecting your own needs for rest and support

Obsessive worry about performance, productivity, or outcome

Anxiety, brooding, or gnawing guilt about responsibilities

Being overly critical and dissatisfied with yourself

Doing others' work for them

It's tempting either to downplay slips—overlooking them as temporary and inconsequential—or to overreact—seeing them as proof of inevitable failure.

Any slip, regardless of how short-lived or situational it seems, must be taken seriously. Agreeing to do something you haven't time or energy for, just this once; getting tied up in knots over a cluttered living room when your in-laws stop by (even though you look perfectly relaxed); not taking time to eat lunch (forget that you could lose a couple of pounds); or running to three different stores to get wrapping paper that matches the birthday card for your lover (since when does he notice?), all constitute slips.

Slips are often used as a way out. When we make a mistake, we feel disheartened. Perhaps changing is too hard, too overwhelming, too much to ask of ourselves, so we give up. "So much for trying! Obviously there's no way to beat this so why make myself miserable?" Sarcasm is another way we talk ourselves out of recovery: "Who needs this? I was better off with all my problems." Rationalizing—coming up with "good" reasons for going back to old behavior—also discounts the significance of slips: "I *had* to stay up all night, three nights in a row, studying. I was sick and blew the midterm, so this is the only way I'm going to get an 'A,'" or, "But it's my parents' fortieth anniversary. Of course I have to throw a lavish party!"

Anything can be an excuse to backslide. Slips are neither meaningless incidents to be swept aside nor reasons to give up the fight. *See slips for what they are:* important clues that you need to strengthen your resolve and continue work on your recovery.

TRIED AND TRUE
SUGGESTIONS FOR
MAXIMIZING
SUCCESS

PUT YOURSELF FIRST

When you embark on a new course, you are faced with making choices. At every turn, there are invitations to ignore, trivialize, procrastinate, or put what you want on the back burner. *Your well-being comes first!* Nothing is more important than your physical, mental, emotional, and spiritual health. It's up to you to make sure nothing interferes or takes precedence over it. Making a balanced life your first priority means taking it seriously. Set aside time and remove anything that impedes or threatens your commitment.

SET FINITE GOALS

Change can seem an insurmountable task. Don't try to tackle everything at once. Work on one thing at a time. Breaking down the steps into exact, finite units keeps you from becoming overwhelmed and increases the likelihood of success. Commit to specific goals, like "Today I will stop working at six o'clock, no matter what," or, "For the next month I will reward myself every time I stop myself from feeling guilty." (And don't feel guilty about the rewards.)

PACE YOURSELF

Perfectionists tend to overestimate themselves. The most famous adage of Alcoholics Anonymous, a saying I've found both true and comforting, is "One day at a time." This statement means that each day presents a new opportunity for working toward your goals; each day you try to do your best; each day begins with a clean slate and ends with the promise of another. Taking one day at a time requires pacing yourself so you don't burn out. This means making changes a little at a time, finding a rhythm that works for you. A day at a time is also an important reminder to live in the present—each day holds all life's possibilities.

DEVELOP EVALUATION TOOLS

How can you tell how you're doing? It's necessary to develop evaluation tools—some basis on which to measure your progress by *your own standards*. The best evaluation tools are ones that clearly determine the criteria at the onset. Some people find an imaginary point system helpful. For example, on a scale of one to ten, a trip to the supermarket without putting on full makeup gets five points. Not taking work home gets eight. Going two days without picking his clothes up gets nine, and so on and so forth. Everyone's point system differs according to what, in her life, represents positive growth. What matters is to find concrete ways of judging your success.

Your feelings are another reliable barometer of how you're doing. If you're peaceful and calm, yet filled with energy, it's likely you're being productive, not a perfectionist. On the other hand, anxiety and unhappiness indicate a continuing struggle.

Note: Resist the urge to compare your progress with anyone else's. Since perfectionists tend to be highly competitive, this is a natural tendency, which should be avoided. The only thing to concern yourself with is your own progress.

BE AWARE OF PITFALLS

Watch out for being overly idealistic. A solid understanding of potential pitfalls helps you to be well-prepared. Four common pitfalls are: COMPLACENCY; BECOMING INSULATED; TRANSFERENCE OF BAD HABITS; and THE "IS THAT ALL THERE IS?" syndrome.

As we become "old hands" at giving up indispensability, it's common to fall prey to complacency. We think we have all the answers. We think we've got it beat. Feelings of complacency are a blinking neon sign that recovery is in danger. Old habits die hard, so it's important to stay alert to relapses.

The second pitfall is becoming so absorbed in making changes—so zealous—that you cut yourself off from the parts of your life that were "problem areas" instead of integrating new behavior into them. Likewise, you might gradually sever relationships with people who aren't on a parallel road, rather than finding new, healthier ways to interact.

A third major pitfall is transferring old, perfectionist habits: no longer making yourself indispensable in one part of your life only to start making yourself indispensable in another, or crossing over to other addictions like chemical dependency, eating disorders, compulsive spending, or sexual addiction. If you only make behavioral changes, without bedrock attitude and value shifts, the underlying issues that led to perfectionism and indispensability will find an outlet in other addictive processes.

"Is that all there is?"—a question universally asked at some point in recovery—signifies an important turning point. This question, sometimes asked with a tinge of sadness, other times in a cynical or belligerent voice, marks the transition between an earlier, more compelling stage of recovery, when each change marks a major triumph, and settling in for the long haul. Fighting the initial battle, a challenge that, like any, excites and stimulates, is followed by normal feelings of letdown.

"Is that all there is?" Yes. And no. Giving up indispensability includes both losses and gains. On the one side you no longer benefit from the payoffs of perfectionism; for many women, the loss of drama, excitement, and heroics is especially missed. On the other side are the beginnings of sanity and the peace that comes from fulfilling needs more directly. Moving into this next, more stable phase of recovery requires grieving the losses, accepting the trade-offs, and opting for more genuine and permanent rewards.

CELEBRATE!

Recovery is difficult. Changing long-standing patterns is painful; the process of shedding old skins is akin to grieving. You must do anything and everything to be loving and patient with yourself.

Active celebration of your successes is the best gift you can possibly give yourself to enhance your recovery. Acknowledge every step—however small—you make toward overcoming the perfection addiction. Notice each time you set limits, ask for support, or choose to protect your energy instead of making yourself indispensable. Every step toward healthier patterns is cause for celebration.

There are many different ways to affirm your progress. The value of joining a support group has been brought up several times in this book. A support group, in which you share struggles and successes alike, is a wonderful way to get a sense of where you've been and where you're going. This can also be done with a close friend, relative, or mate.

Keeping a written record of your goals is a way to track how you're doing. Marking significant anniversaries (six months of not giving in and volunteering for extra assignments!) is another way to formally recognize your successes and cheer yourself on. Since recovery is an ongoing, life-long proposition, after a while it can be hard to see how far you've come. For this reason, I urge you to take note of all gains and reward yourself for your hard work.

If the idea of recovery seems too serious for someone with problems like yours, remember: Things that don't get better, get worse. Taken to its extreme, the consequences of indispensability are reduced coping, physical illness, emotional trauma, impaired relationships, and spiritual despair.

If the idea of recovery seems overwhelming, remember: Small steps are all that's required; only take on what you can comfortably deal with and take your time.

If recovery seems to demand a great deal of energy, more than you wish to expend, remember: You are already putting out huge sums of energy making yourself indispensable. Why not use the same energy to take care of yourself and improve the quality of your life?

MOVING BEYOND PERFECTIONISM

Beyond perfectionism is something better, something healthier and more gratifying. Giving yourself permission to be a full human being—nothing more, nothing less—frees you to fulfill your potential and make important, exciting, life-altering changes.

When you stop making yourself indispensable, you begin to pay attention to your physical health. Over time, energy is restored, your resistance builds, and your overall stamina and well-being radically improve.

When you stop making yourself indispensable you get *more* done. Instead of squandering your energy and running around in circles, you're able to focus and concentrate on what interests you most. Your level of awareness is heightened and you may discover a "calling" or develop long-neglected talents and gifts.

When you stop making yourself indispensable, you ask for, welcome, and openly appreciate participation and support; relationships with people interested in equality will deepen and grow. People in your life don't have to live up to your perfectionistic standards anymore. Instead of controlling them, you are more able to accept them as they are. Your sense of humor returns. Sexuality and intimacy become infinitely more satisfying.

When you stop making yourself indispensable, you open yourself to the possibility of spiritual connection and nourishment. Rather than seeing yourself as responsible for everything, you perceive a higher power, a larger plan in which you have a unique and special role. There is a gradual metamorphosis: from inadequacy to humility, from grandiosity to honest appreciation of who you are and what you have to give.

I haven't completely stopped making myself indispensable, but I'm a lot closer. I'm less likely to panic when everything isn't finished—instantly, perfectly, exactly to my liking. I no longer feel as if everything is exclusively in my hands, and I'm more willing to receive help and support. I'm working at achieving balance— allowing myself "down time"; making plans for Gary and me to spend special, uninterrupted time together rather than fitting our relationship around paying bills and making lunches; making it a priority to reconnect with friends; and savoring my children without worrying so much about the time we're apart. Mostly, I'm discovering the relief and pleasure of living my life as best I can, rather than always trying to live up to some imaginary, unreachable standard.

Self-acceptance is the ultimate goal of overcoming the addiction to perfection. You know you're on the way when, instead of making yourself indispensable, you simply want to give what you can. You know you're on the right road when, instead of trying to be perfect, you know, really know in your heart, that your best is the most anyone can ask for. Your best is truly enough.

CHAPTER NOTES

Chapter one

1. Herbert J. Freudenberger and Gail North, *Women's Burnout*, Doubleday, New York, 1985.
2. Sylvia Ann Hewlett, *A Lesser Life: The Myth of Women's Liberation in America*, Morrow, New York, 1986.
3. Ellen Sue Stern, *Expecting Change: The Emotional Journey Through Pregnancy*, Poseidon Press/Simon & Schuster, New York, 1986.
4. Barbara J. Berg, *The Crisis of the Working Mother: Resolving the Conflict Between Family and Work*, Summit Books, New York, 1986, p. 27.
5. Grace K. Baruch, *Lifeprints*, McGraw-Hill, New York, 1983.

Chapter three

1. Linda Tschirhart Sanford and Mary Ellen Donovan, *Women and Self-Esteem: Understanding and Improving the Way We Think and Feel About Ourselves*, Penguin Books, New York, 1984, p. 310.

Chapter four

1. Arthur Janov, *The Primal Scream*, Putnam Books, New York, 1970.

2. Nancy Chodorow, "Family Structure and Feminine Personality." In M. Z. Rosaldo and L. Lamphere, eds., *Woman, Culture and Society*. Stanford University Press, Stanford, 1974.

3. Jean Baker Miller, M.D., *Toward a New Psychology of Women*, Beacon Press, Boston, 1976, p. 62.

4. Colette Dowling, *The Cinderella Complex: Women's Hidden Fear of Independence*, Pocket Books, New York, 1981.

5. Nancy Friday, *My Mother/Myself,* Delacorte Press, New York, 1977.

6. Robert J. Stoller, "A Contribution to the Study of Gender Identity." *International Journal of Psycho-Analysis* 45 (1964): 220–26.

7. Myra and David Sadker, "Sexism in the Classroom." *Vocational Education Journal* (October 1985).

8. Hilda Scott, *Working Your Way to the Bottom: The Feminization of Poverty*, Pandora Press, London, England, 1984.

9. Marabel Morgan, *The Total Woman,* F. H. Revell, Old Tappan, New Jersey, 1973.

10. Martha T. Schuch Mednick and Hilda J. Weissman, "The Psychology of Women-Selected Topics." *Female Psychology: The Emerging Self,* Science Research Associates, 1976.

11. *The Wall Street Journal,* Eastern Edition, February 6, 1986, p. 25.

12. Torben Vestergaard and Kim Schroder, *The Language of Advertising,* Basil Blackwell, Oxford, 1985, p. 79.

13. Ad Dollar Summary, January–September, 1986, Leading National Advertisers, New York.

14. Bernard P. Prusak, "Woman: Seductive Siren and Source of Sin." In Rosemary Radford Ruether, ed., *Religion and Sexism: Images of Woman in the Jewish and Christian Traditions*, Simon & Schuster, New York, 1974.

15. Judith Hauptman, "Images of Women in the Talmud." In Rosemary Radford Ruether, ed., *Religion and Sexism: Images of Woman in the Jewish and Christian Traditions,* Simon & Schuster, New York, 1974.

16. Ibid., p. 191.

17. Jan Magrane, *Haunted by the Holy Ghost*. Produced by At the Foot of the Mountain Theatre, Minneapolis, March, 1983.

Chapter five

1. M. Scott Peck, *The Road Less Traveled: A New Psychology of Love, Traditional Values and Spiritual Growth*, Simon & Schuster, New York, 1978.
2. Sanford and Donovan, op. cit., p. 7.
3. U.S. Department of Commerce, *Current Population Report: Money Income of Households, Families, and Persons in the United States: 1984*, Washington, D.C., April 1986.
4. Hewlett, op. cit., p. 71.
5. Hewlett, op. cit., p. 13.
6. Hewlett, op. cit., p. 66.
7. Judith Viorst, *Necessary Losses: The Loves, Illusions, Dependencies and Impossible Expectations That All of Us Have to Give Up in Order to Grow*, Simon & Schuster, New York, 1986, p. 30.
8. Robin Norwood, *Women Who Love Too Much: When you keep wishing and hoping he'll change*, Jeremy P. Tarcher, Los Angeles, 1985.
9. Viorst, op. cit., p. 182.
10. Vernon E. Johnson, *I'll Quit Tomorrow*, Harper & Row, New York, 1973.

Chapter six

1. Dennis T. Jaffee, Ph.D., *Healing from Within: Psychological Techniques to Help the Mind Heal the Body*, Simon & Schuster, New York, 1980, Chapter Three.
2. Dr. Robert Eliot, *Is It Worth Dying For?*, Bantam Books, New York, 1984.
3. Norma Rosen, "Hers" column of January 1983, reprinted in *Hers: Through Women's Eyes*, Harper & Row (Perennial Library), New York, 1986, p. 75.

4. Women account for one in five cardiac patients—American Heart Association, 1-800-527-6941.

5. Incidence of substance abuse in women—National Council on Alcoholism, (212) 206-6770.

6. Norwood, op. cit., p. 164.

Chapter seven

1. William Bridges, Ph.D., *Transitions: Making Sense of Life's Changes*, Addison-Wesley, Reading, Massachusetts, 1980, pp. 90–104.

2. Portia Nelson, *Poem in Five Chapters*. Reprinted from *Repeat After Me*, Claudia Black, M.A.C. Book Department, Denver, Colorado, p. 10.

3. The term "white knuckling" is often used as part of the informal vernacular of twelve-step programs.

Chapter eight

1. The Alcoholics Anonymous's Twelve Steps to recovery are as follows:

 1. We admitted we were powerless over alcohol—that our lives had become unmanageable.
 2. Came to believe that a Power greater than ourselves could restore us to sanity.
 3. Made a decision to turn our will and our lives over to the care of God as we understood Him.
 4. Made a searching and fearless moral inventory of ourselves.
 5. Admitted to God, ourselves, and to another human being the exact nature of our wrongs.
 6. Were entirely ready to have God remove all these defects of character.
 7. Humbly asked Him to remove our shortcomings.
 8. Made a list of all persons we had harmed, and became willing to make amends to all of them.

9. Made direct amends to such people wherever possible, except when to do so would injure them or others.

10. Continued to take personal inventory and when we were wrong promptly admitted it.

11. Sought through prayer and meditation to improve our conscious contact with God as we understood Him, praying only for knowledge of His will for us and the power to carry that out.

12. Having had a spiritual awakening as the result of these steps, we tried to carry this message to alcoholics, and to practice these principles in all our affairs.

The Twelve Steps reprinted with permission of Alcoholics Anonymous World Services, Inc.

2. See Appendix I, "How to Start Your Own Support Group"; *Women Who Love Too Much,* Robin Norwood.

3. Viorst, op. cit., pp. 132–33.

4. Dr. Seuss, *The Cat in the Hat,* Random House, New York, 1957.

READING LIST

Here is a list of books I strongly recommend. They are all related to the subject of perfectionism and are organized by category.

Psychology

Jean Miller Baker, M.D., *Toward a New Psychology of Women*, second edition, Beacon Press, Boston, 1986
  This concise, well-written book does a wonderful job of describing female conditioning and putting it within a social and political framework. Chapter Six, "Serving Others' Needs," is especially relevant.

Harriet Goldhor Lerner, Ph.D., *The Dance of Anger: A Woman's Guide to Changing the Patterns of Intimate Relationships*, Harper & Row, New York, 1985
  A warm and personal exploration of the causes and patterns of anger. Includes strategies for change.

Carol Gilligan, *In a Different Voice: Psychological Theory and Women's Development*, Harvard University Press, Cambridge, Massachusetts, 1982
  Gilligan's groundbreaking book on the differences between male and female development helps us understand why women tend to be more empathetic and other-oriented. Written in a highly

academic tone, the book takes some concentration to read, but is well worth it.

Luise Eichenbaum and Susie Orbach, *Between Women: Love, Envy, and Competition in Women's Friendships,* Viking Penguin Inc., New York, 1988
Written by two internationally acclaimed psychotherapists, this warm and intelligent book focuses on indispensability between women friends, and its consequences.

Jean Shinoda Bolen, M.D., *Goddesses in Everywoman: A New Psychology of Women,* Harper & Row, New York, 1985
This well-researched book presents an alternative vision of women, using seven archetypal goddesses or personality types. Very positive and affirming.

Maggie Scarf, *Unfinished Business: Pressure Points in the Lives of Women,* Ballantine Books, New York, 1980
A rich and detailed account of the causes of depression and turning points in women's lives. Very instructive and enjoyable reading.

Colette Dowling, *The Cinderella Complex: Women's Hidden Fear of Independence,* Pocket Books, New York, 1981
An earlier book that continues to be relevant, *The Cinderella Complex* explores female dependency and ambivalence about taking charge of our lives.

Linda Tschirhart Sanford and Mary Ellen Donovan, *Women and Self-Esteem: Understanding and Improving the Way We Think and Feel About Ourselves,* Penguin Books, New York, 1985
Both anecdotal and very concrete, this no-nonsense book does a good job of outlining the sources of low self-esteem in women and offers tools for building confidence.

Susan Brownmiller, *Femininity,* Fawcett Columbia, New York, 1984

Each chapter in this wonderfully interesting book concentrates on a specific aspect of femininity. It reads almost like a collection of short stories.

Addiction

Anne Wilson Schaef, *Society Becomes an Addict,* Harper & Row, San Francisco, 1987

An examination of the prevalence of the addictive process in contemporary society, this book helps put indispensability in context. Schaef's first book, *Women's Reality,* a primer in feminism, is also essential reading.

Melody Beattie, *Codependent No More: How to Stop Controlling Others and Start Caring for Yourself,* Hazeldon Foundation/ Harper & Row, Minneapolis, 1987

The most useful and accessible book on co-dependency I've found. Beattie does a great job describing the problem in everyday language and offers real hope for change.

Claudia Black, *Repeat After Me,* M.A.C. Book Department, Denver, Colorado, 1985

More of a workbook, this is a worthwhile, hands-on approach to combating co-dependency.

Kim Chernin, *The Obsession: Reflections on the Tyranny of Slenderness,* Harper & Row, New York, 1981

A perceptive study of society's insistence that women be thin. Chernin's second book, *The Hungry Self,* explores eating disorders in the context of women's struggle for identity. Both books are valuable reading.

Motherhood

Angela Barron McBride, *The Growth and Development of Mothers,* Harper & Row, New York, 1973

A bit simplistic and dated in tone, this book nonetheless lays the groundwork for serious consideration of the stresses and challenges of motherhood.

Barbara J. Berg, *The Crisis of the Working Mother: Resolving the Conflict Between Family and Work*, Summit Books, New York, 1986

A much-needed, well-written examination of the inner conflict experienced by women trying to balance family and career responsibilities. Chapter Two includes an excellent discussion on the origins of guilt.

Adrienne Rich, *Of Woman Born: Motherhood as Experience and Institution*, Bantam Books, New York, 1977

A classic study on the role of women in society. Rich's poetic and deeply personal insight rests on a solid foundation of academic scholarship.

Anita Shreve, *Remaking Motherhood: How Working Mothers Are Shaping Our Children's Future*, Viking Penguin, New York, 1987

A worthwhile attempt at countering the assumption that children necessarily suffer from being in day-care. This book reframes the traditional concept of motherhood and tries for a more contemporary, realistic vision.

Lucy Freeman and Herbert S. Strean, *Guilt—Letting Go*, Wiley, New York, 1986

As the title suggests, this book explores letting go of guilt. Warmly written, it provides a working definition of guilt and offers tangible suggestions for accepting our own limitations.

Lynn Caine, *What Did I Do Wrong?: Mothers, Children, Guilt*, Arbor House, New York, 1985

An easy-reading book that reminds mothers that they are *not* responsible for everything that happens to their children. Very supportive.

Politics and sexism

Torben Vestergaard and Kim Schroder, *The Language of Advertising,* Basil Blackwell, Oxford, 1985

A revealing study of the underlying messages present in advertising. Chapter Four specifically addresses the cultural images of women reinforced through the media.

Dorothy Dinnerstein, *The Mermaid and the Minotaur: Sexual Arrangements and Human Malaise,* Harper & Row, New York, 1976

An intellectually challenging discussion of the sexual arrangements between men and women. Dinnerstein combines myth, anthropology, and psychology in analyzing the deeper layers of social conditioning.

Robin Tolmach Lakoff and Raquell Scherr, *Face Value: The Politics of Beauty,* Routledge and Kegan Paul, Boston, 1984

A terrific explanation of the relationship between political structure and the inner pressure to conform to a cultural image of beauty.

Wendy Chapkis, *Beauty Secrets: Women and the Politics of Success,* South End Press, Boston, 1986

This radical book shakes up our images of female beauty and success.

Sylvia Ann Hewlett, *A Lesser Life: The Myth of Women's Liberation in America,* Morrow, New York, 1986

An impressive and sobering discussion of the lack of support available to women in American society. Bulky but worthwhile.

Themes of perfectionism and overachievement

Harriet B. Braiker, Ph.D., *The Type "E" Woman: How to Overcome the Stress of Being Everything to Everybody,* Dodd, Mead, New York, 1986

Concrete strategies for stopping the compulsion to be "Superwoman," based on the author's clinical experience as a therapist.

Gail North and Herbert Freudenberger, *Women's Burnout*, Doubleday, New York, 1985
An excellent overview of the symptoms and solutions of combating burnout. A convincing description of the effects of stress in our lives.

Gershen Kaufman, *Shame—The Power of Caring*, Schenkman Books, Cambridge, Massachusetts, 1980
An important study of how feelings of shame keep us isolated and reinforce our need to gain others' approval. Scholarly, yet written in very human language.

Robin Norwood, *Women Who Love Too Much: When you keep wishing and hoping he'll change*, Jeremy P. Tarcher, Los Angeles, 1985
A powerful exploration of addictive love relationships between women and men. A life-changing book.

Judith Viorst, *Necessary Losses: The Loves, Illusions, Dependencies and Impossible Expectations That All of Us Have to Give Up in Order to Grow*, Simon & Schuster, New York, 1986
Based on Freudian theory, this bestseller focuses on the theme of letting go—from birth to death and everything in between. Stylish and intelligent, Viorst educates while she entertains.

William Bridges, *Transitions: Making Sense of Life's Changes*, Addison-Wesley, Reading, Massachusetts, 1980
Warm and anecdotal, this book introduces the idea of natural life transitions. Bridges helps the reader understand how traumatic events can be positive turning points.

Linda and Richard Eyre, *Lifebalance: Bringing Harmony to Your Everyday Life,* Ballantine Books, New York, 1987

A guide for integrating life's competing responsibilities, with the goal of attaining a more peaceful existence. Written in a workbook style, *Lifebalance* tends toward an evangelical tone, but is still food for thought.

Women and religion

Rosemary Radford Ruether, editor, *Religion and Sexism: Images of Woman in the Jewish and Christian Traditions,* Simon & Schuster, New York, 1974

An excellent anthology of writings regarding the impact of Judeo-Christian religious teachings on women's psyches.

Mary Daly, *Beyond God the Father: Toward a Philosophy of Women's Liberation,* Beacon Press, Boston, 1973

An impassioned, highly intellectual study of the patriarchal roots of Christianity; proposes a new spirituality based on authentic female images.

ABOUT THE AUTHOR

Ellen Sue Stern, nationally known speaker, founder of Expecting Change workshops, and faculty member of the Institute of Integral Development, has helped thousands of women and men in their recovery from indispensability. Her work has appeared in such national magazines as *New Woman, Self, Parenting,* and *Woman's Day.* She lives in Minneapolis with her husband, Gary, and their children, Zoe and Evan.

BANTAM BOOKS
ON ADDICTION AND RECOVERY

ADDICTION

The most up-to-date information from the leading experts in the field.

RESTORE YOUR LIFE
A Living Plan for Sober People
Anne Geller, M.D. with M.J. Territo
From one of this country's leading medical experts on addiction, this is the most comprehensive guide available to physical, emotional, and mental health in sobriety. For recovering alcoholics and drug addicts, the book features meal plans, exercise programs, and more.
07153-X • *Hardcover* • $21.95/$26.95 in Canada

800-COCAINE
Mark S. Gold, M.D.
From the leading expert on cocaine abuse and treatment, an informative, prescriptive manual with hard facts on America's fastest growing drug problem.
34388-2 • *Large Format Paperback* • $3.50/$3.95 in Canada

THE FACTS ABOUT DRUGS AND ALCOHOL
Mark S. Gold, M.D.
The bestselling author of 800-COCAINE provides concise, medically proven information on marijuana, heroin, LSD, crack, and other commonly abused substances.
27826-6 • *Paperback* • $3.95/$4.95 in Canada

UNDER THE INFLUENCE
A Guide to the Myths and Realities of Alcoholism
James R. Milam, Ph.D., and Katherine Ketcham
This groundbreaking classic emphasizes treating alcoholism as a physiological disease and offers information on how to tell if someone is an alcoholic, treatment, and recovery.
27487-2 • *Paperback* • $4.95/$5.95 in Canada

RECOVERY

From alcoholism to eating disorders, books that offer concrete tools for physical, emotional and spiritual recovery.

HOMECOMING
Reclaiming and Championing Your Inner Child
John Bradshaw
As seen in the nationally televised PBS series, this bestselling book presents the essence of the inner child workshop John Bradshaw calls "the most powerful work I have ever done," a step-by-step guide to healing the wounds of the past and discovering your true self.
05793-6 • *Hardcover* • $18.95/$23.95 in Canada

DON'T CALL IT LOVE
Recovery from Sexual Addiction
Patrick Carnes, Ph.D.
From the nation's leading expert on sexual addiction, author of *Out of the Shadows* and *Contrary to Love*, comes this extraordinary documentary look at the nature and causes of sexual addiction, plus healing advice from more than 1000 men and women in advanced recovery.
07236-6 • *Hardcover* • $19.95/$24.95 in Canada

LIVING ON THE EDGE
A Guide to Intervention for Families with Drug and Alcohol Problems
Katherine Ketcham and Ginny Lyford Gustafson
From two renowned professionals, compassionate, step-by-step advice on every facet of family intervention, from preparation to finding the right treatment options and support groups.
34606-7 • *Large Format Paperback* • $7.95/$9.95 in Canada

RECOVERING
How to Get and Stay Sober
L. Ann Mueller, M.D., and Katherine Ketcham
An essential resource for alcoholics and those who love them, a comprehensive and compassionate guide to new treatment programs that have helped many alcoholics achieve lasting sobriety.
34303-3 • *Large Format Paperback* • $8.95/$11.95 in Canada

RECLAIMING OUR LIVES
Hope for Adult Survivors of Incest
Carol Poston and Karen Lison
A comprehensive, inspiring, and supportive guide with a concrete, 14-step program for healing by an incest survivor and a therapist.
34778-0 • *Large Format Paperback* • $9.95/$12.95 in Canada

THE TWELVE STEPS REVISITED
Ronald L. Rogers, Chandler Scott McMillin, Morris A. Hill
An inspiring new interpretation of the 12 steps of Alcoholics Anonymous that clearly illustrates the path toward recovery that has worked for so many millions of people.
34733-0 • *Large Format Paperback* • $7.95/$9.95 in Canada

DON'T HELP
A Positive Guide to Working with the Alcoholic
Ronald L. Rogers and Chandler Scott McMillin
For counselors, health-care professionals, and families, a definitive and practical guide to working with the alcoholic.
34716-0 • *Large Format Paperback* • $8.95/$11.95 in Canada

ADULT CHILDREN
Essential reading for the millions who grew up in dysfunctional families.

THE ADULT CHILDREN OF ALCOHOLICS SYNDROME
Wayne Kritsberg
Real help and hope for adult children in a complete self-help program that shows how to recognize and remedy the effects of the dysfunctional family.
27279-9 • *Paperback* • $3.95/$4.95 in Canada

BECOMING YOUR OWN PARENT
The Solution for Adult Children of Alcoholic and Other Dysfunctional Families
Dennis Wholey
Television host Dennis Wholey, author of *The Courage to Change* and himself an "adult child," takes us inside a series of meetings where fourteen men and women learn to find within themselves the validation and nurturance they were denied as children. Also offers

the wisdom of a dozen nationally recognized experts on recovery.
34788-8 • *Large Format Paperback* • $9.95/$12.95 in Canada

HEALING FOR ADULT CHILDREN OF ALCOHOLICS
Sara Hines Martin
A groundbreaking work that examines the spiritual and emotional healing that must take place for complete recovery from the ACOA Syndrome.
"Truly commendable"—Dr. Robert H. Schuller
28246-8 • *Paperback* • $4.50/$5.50 in Canada

POTATO CHIPS FOR BREAKFAST
The True Story of Growing Up in an Alcoholic Family
Cynthia Scales
The shocking true story of a young girl who grew up with every material comfort—and two alcoholic parents.
28166-6 • *Paperback* • $3.95/$4.95 in Canada

FAMILY ISSUES
Groundbreaking books on conquering co-dependence and helping addicted family members.

LOVING AN ALCOHOLIC
Help and Hope for Co-dependents
Jack Mumey
The founder of the Gateway Treatment Center for alcoholics and their families presents practical advice—a way out of confusion and pain, and past roadblocks to change.
27236-5 • *Paperback* • $4.50/$5.50 in Canada

ADDICTED TO ADULTERY
How We Saved Our Marriage
How You Can Save Yours
Richard and Elizabeth Brzeczek and Sharon De Vita
The former Chicago police superintendent and his wife discuss how infidelity nearly destroyed their marriage, and how they formed WESOM (We Saved Our Marriage), the first self-help group for married couples devastated by adultery, featuring the 12-Step Relationship Recovery Program.
05397-3 • *Hardcover* • $17.95/$21.95 in Canada

TOXIC PARENTS
Overcoming Their Hurtful Legacy and Reclaiming Your Life
Dr. Susan Forward with Craig Buck
The challenging compassionate, and controversial new guide to recognizing and recovering from the lasting damage caused by physical or emotional abuse in childhood, by the best-selling author of *Men Who Hate Women and the Women Who Love Them*.
05700-6 • *Hardcover* • $18.95/$23.95 in Canada

HEALING RELATIONSHIPS
Books that point readers toward a healthier self and new ways of relating with others.

HOW TO BREAK YOUR ADDICTION TO A PERSON
Howard M. Halpern, Ph.D.
An insightful, step-by-step guide to breaking painful addictive relationships—and surviving separation.
23874-4 • *Paperback* • $3.95/$4.95 in Canada

OUT OF DARKNESS INTO THE LIGHT
A Journey of Inner Healing
Gerald G. Jampolsky, M.D.
The bestselling author of *Love Is Letting Go of Fear* offers a blueprint for recovery through his personal journey from severe depression, guilt, and alcohol abuse to a triumphant rediscovery of self and inner healing.
05350-7 • *Hardcover* • $14.95/$18.95 in Canada

BECOMING NATURALLY THERAPEUTIC
A Return to the True Essence of Helping
Jacquelyn Small
The renowned workshop leader's inspiring guide for all who serve as listeners or counselors in the lives of others. Basing her work on landmark studies, Small helps us "straight-talk" beyond our co-dependent or controlling ways of helping others and teaches how to offer clear and loving guidance directly from the heart.
34800-0 • *Large Format Paper* • $7.95/$9.95 in Canada

MEDITATIONALS

Daily inspiration and guidance based on the 12-step programs.

A NEW DAY
365 Meditations for Personal and Spiritual Growth
Anonymous
Offers spiritual and psychological guidance on overcoming the struggles we face each day, by the author of *A Day at a Time*.
34591-5 • *Paperback* • $6.95/$8.95 in Canada

FAMILY FEELINGS
Daily Meditations for Healthy Relationships
Martha Vanceburg and Sylvia Silverman
Valuable insights on changing destructive family patterns with one's spouse, children, elderly parents, and grandparents. By the co-author of *The Promise of a New Day* and her mother.
34705-5 • *Paperback* • $6.95/$8.95 in Canada

A TIME TO BE FREE
Daily Meditations for Enhancing Self-Esteem
Anonymous
By the bestselling author of *A New Day* and *A Day at a Time,* a new kind of daily meditational that offers insight into 52 issues as well as providing the steps that can be taken to achieve the freedom to be your best self.
35203-2 • *Paperback* • $7.95/$9.95 in Canada